NATIONS *IN TRANSITION*

IRELAND

New and future titles in the
Nations in Transition series include:

China

India

Indonesia

Iran

North Korea

Pakistan

Russia

South Korea

Vietnam

NATIONS *IN TRANSITION*

IRELAND

by Russell Roberts

GREENHAVEN PRESS
SAN DIEGO, CALIFORNIA

THOMSON

GALE

Detroit • New York • San Diego • San Francisco
Boston • New Haven, Conn. • Waterville, Maine
London • Munich

Library of Congress Cataloging-in-Publication Data

Roberts, Russell, 1953–
Ireland / by Russell Roberts.
p. cm. — (Nations in transition)
Includes bibliographical references (p.   ) and index.
Contents: A nation defined by struggle—The troubles—The partition
of Ireland—The Irish Republic—Trouble begins again—New hope
for peace?
ISBN 0-7377-1094-2 (hardback : alk. paper)
1. Ireland—Juvenile literature. [1. Ireland—History.] I. Title.
II. Series.
DA906 .R63 2002
941.5—dc21

2001007282

Copyright © 2002 by Greenhaven Press,
an imprint of The Gale Group
10911 Technology Place, San Diego, CA 92127
Printed in the U.S.A.

Contents

Foreword   6
Introduction
   A Land of Contrasts   8

Chapter One
   A Nation Defined by Struggle   10

Chapter Two
   Battles for Independence   28

Chapter Three
   Birth of Two Nations   43

Chapter Four
   Making Independence Work   59

Chapter Five
   Renewed Conflict   75

Chapter Six
   Ireland at a Crossroad   87

   Notes   98
   Chronology   100
   For Further Reading   104
   Works Consulted   105
   Index   107
   Picture Credits   112
   About the Author   112

Foreword

In 1986 Soviet general secretary Mikhail Gorbachev initiated his plan to reform the economic, political, and social structure of the Soviet Union. Nearly three-quarters of a century of Communist ideology was dismantled in the next five years. As the totalitarian regime relaxed its rule and opened itself up to the West, the Soviet peoples clamored for more freedoms. Hard-line Communists resisted Gorbachev's lead, but glasnost, or "openness," could not be stopped with the will of the common people behind it.

In 1991 the changing USSR held its first multicandidate elections. The reform-minded Boris Yeltsin, a supporter of Gorbachev, became the first popularly elected president of the Russian Republic in Soviet history. Under Yeltsin's leadership, the old Communist policies soon all but disintegrated, as did the Soviet Union itself. The Union of Soviet Socialist Republics broke apart into fifteen independent entities. The former republics reformed into a more democratic union now referred to as the Commonwealth of Independent States. Russia remained the nominal figurehead of the commonwealth, but it no longer dictated the future of the other independent states.

By the new millennium, Russia and the other commonwealth states still faced crises. The new states were all in transition from decades of totalitarian rule to the postglasnost era of unprecedented and untested democratic reforms. Revamping the Soviet economy may have opened up new opportunities in private ownership of property and business, but it did not bring overnight prosperity to the former republics. Common necessities such as food still remain in short supply in many regions. And while new governments seek to stabilize their authority, crime rates have escalated throughout the former Soviet Union. Still, the people are confident that their newfound freedoms—freedom of speech and assembly, freedom of religion, and even the right of workers to strike—will ultimately better their lives. The process of change will take time and the people are willing to see their respective states through the challenges of this transitional period in Soviet history.

The collapse and rebuilding of the former Soviet Union provides perhaps the best example of a contemporary "nation in transition," the focus of this Greenhaven Press series. However, other nations that fall under the series rubric have faced a host of unique and varied cultural shifts. India, for instance, is a stable, guiding force in Asia, yet it remains a nation in transition more than fifty years after winning independence from Great Britain. The entire infrastructure of the Indian subcontinent still bears the marking of its colonial past: In a land of eighteen official spoken languages, for example, English remains the voice of politics and education. India is still coming to grips with its colonial legacy while forging its place as a strong player in Asian and world affairs.

North Korea's place in Greenhaven's Nations in Transition series is based on major recent political developments. After decades of antagonism between its Communist government and the democratic leadership of South Korea, tensions seemed to ease in the late 1990s. Even under the shadow of the North's developing nuclear capabilities, the presidents of both North and South Korea met in 2000 to propose plans for possible reunification of the two estranged nations. And though it is one of the three remaining bastions of communism in the world, North Korea is choosing not to remain an isolated relic of the Cold War. While it has not earned the trust of the United States and many of its Western allies, North Korea has begun to reach out to its Asian neighbors to encourage trade and cultural exchanges.

These three countries exemplify the types of changes and challenges that qualify them as subjects of study in the Greenhaven Nations in Transition series. The series examines specific nations to disclose the major social, political, economic, and cultural shifts that have caused massive change and in many cases, brought about regional and/or worldwide shifts in power. Detailed maps, inserts, and pictures help flesh out the people, places, and events that define the country's transitional period. Furthermore, a comprehensive bibliography points readers to other sources that will deepen their understanding of the nation's complex past and contemporary struggles. With these tools, students and casual readers trace both past history and future challenges of these important nations.

Introduction

A Land of Contrasts

Ireland is a country of contrasts: green and seemingly peaceful, inhabited by a friendly people who tend their farms, hang out their wash to dry, and gather at pubs to talk over the latest agricultural prices. But Ireland is also a country in which some of the people plant bombs in cars, shoulder rifles at the first opportunity, and, when they gather at the pubs, are just as likely to fervently argue over religion as they are to casually discuss the price of corn.

Violence in Irish politics is an old and all-too-common occurrence. Many attempts have been made to find peace for that troubled land, only to have each and every attempt dashed by religious extremism.

Although Ireland is a relatively small country, it has a significant impact in the world, particularly on the nations of Europe. The violence in Northern Ireland and the attempts to suppress it impose a significant burden on Britain. Furthermore, the Republic of Ireland's goal of participating in a unified Europe depends on a peaceful settlement of Northern Ireland's conflicts.

Achieving peace almost certainly will require all Irish to make some accommodations. Citizens of the republic have for decades longed for the day when their nation will be reunited with the neighboring six counties of Northern Ireland, but they are faced with the reality that a majority of the citizens of the north oppose reunification. For their part, Northern Ireland's citizens, who are British subjects, are facing up to the fact that a sizable minority ardently desires some sort of political affiliation with its southern neighbor, if not complete reunification.

In a world that is growing evermore interconnected, Ireland's role on the world stage will only increase in the future.

Irish children look forward to a peaceful future.

Moreover, learning who the Irish are, and learning about the roots of the conflicts that wrack what is poetically termed the Emerald Isle, may aid in understanding similar conflicts elsewhere in the world.

This book is the story of Ireland—a land of contrasts and certainly a nation in transition.

A Nation Defined by Struggle

1

The partition of Ireland in 1921 set the stage for the current unrest in Northern Ireland, where Catholics who want to join the Irish republic and Protestants who want to remain part of the United Kingdom engage in vicious guerrilla warfare to gain supremacy for their point of view. Yet the conflict actually dates back many centuries, and violence in Irish politics is a long-standing phenomenon.

Much of what people think of as Irish culture actually originated elsewhere, arriving in 500 B.C. with the Celts, who came from Gaul, which later would comprise France, Belgium, and northern Italy. In modern times, in fact, experts refer to these invaders as Gaelic Celts. As the years passed, the Gaelic Celts became the dominant culture on the island. The peoples the Celts conquered retreated to remote hilltops and boggy areas that were of little interest to the newcomers.

Ireland Gets Its Name

The first culture that the Celts encountered and conquered when they arrived were the Eirann, who were living in the southern part of the island. It was from the Eirann that the Celts devised the name of the island: Eire, or Erin.

Eventually Gaelic Ireland evolved into a series of some 150 small autonomous kingdoms called *tuaths*. Around the fourth century, however, many of these kingdoms combined, and Ireland became divided into five kingdoms: Meath, Leinster, Munster, Connacht, and Ulster.

The bulk of Ireland's population consisted of peasants who eked out a meager living on their small plots of land. At this time, most Irishmen had a relationship with the lord who owned the land they lived on that was more important than the relationship with their family. The relationship varied, depending on whether the peasant was a free client or a base client. If a man was a free client, he was granted some livestock by his lord and was allowed to work his own small plot of land. In return, he was expected to supply the lord with a specific amount of produce and other products at the end of the farming season. However, if a man was a base client, he owed his lord a certain amount of unpaid physical labor in addition to the agricultural products. Base clients might never rise above that level. With luck, however, free clients might accumulate enough livestock so that they could lend it out and thus make others their clients.

Christianity Comes to Ireland

For centuries the Irish lived undisturbed in this way. Then, in A.D. 401, although the implications were unknown at the time, an event that would forever mark the people of Ireland occurred, when Palladius, a French deacon, was sent to Ireland by Pope Celestine to convert the Irish from their pagan religion.

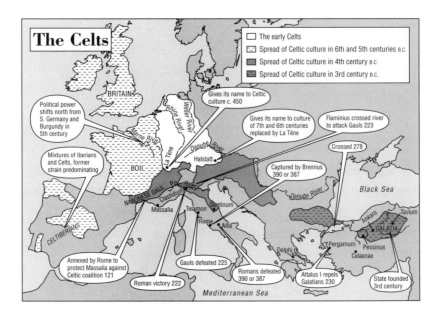

The Celts

- The early Celts
- Spread of Celtic culture in 6th and 5th centuries B.C.
- Spread of Celtic culture in 4th century B.C.
- Spread of Celtic culture in 3rd century B.C.

Political power shifts north from S. Germany and Burgundy in 5th century

Mixtures of Iberians and Celts, former strain predominating

BRITAIN

Gives its name to Celtic culture c. 450

Gives its name to culture of 7th and 6th centuries replaced by La Téne

Flaminius crossed river to attack Gauls 223

Crossed 278

Captured by Brennus 390 or 387

Black Sea

BOII

Halstatt

Weser River

Rhine River

Marne River

La Téne

Danube River

NARBONESE GAUL

Clastidium

Massalia

Telamon

Sentinum

Rome

Allia

Po River

Danube River

Ankara

Tavium

GALATIA

CELTIBERIANS

Delphi

Pergamum

Pessinus

Celaenae

Annexed by Rome to protect Massalia against Celtic coalition 121

Gauls defeated 225

Roman victory 222

Romans defeated 390 or 387

Attalus I repels Galatians 230

State founded 3rd century

Mediterranean Sea

St. Patrick

Although he is the patron saint of Ireland, St. Patrick's life is shrouded in mystery. Much of what modern scholars know about him comes from two documents he wrote, the *Letter to the Soldiers of Coroticus* and the *Confession*. Some scholars believe that Patrick was born in A.D. 415, the son of a deacon and minor official named Calpurnius, who had a country estate, possibly on the island of Anglesey located in Northwestern Wales. These same scholars believe that Patrick did not give much thought to his religion until he was captured and taken into slavery by Irish pirates. Once a slave in northern Ireland, he turned to his faith and began to pray. One day he heard a voice telling him to escape.

Saint Patrick (center) helped establish Christianity in Ireland.

After escaping his captors and returning home to Britain, he had a dream in which a multitude of voices begged him to preach to the Irish. Patrick also felt called to become a priest. After he was ordained, Patrick returned to Ireland, probably in 432. There, he helped establish Christianity. Patrick remained in Ireland until his death in 461.

As a result of Palladius's efforts, Christianity gradually overspread the island.

Through the eighth century A.D., learning in Ireland flourished. In large measure, this was because of Christianity's influence; thanks to the many monasteries established since Palladius had first arrived, Ireland had become a land where a substantial number of people were literate. The Irish, in fact, were widely respected for that quality. So identified were the Irish with literacy that it was said during this time that any man who could read Greek must have been educated in Ireland. Because of the close relationship between learning and religion, Ireland was nicknamed "the Island of Saints and Scholars."[1]

The Arrival of the English

Ireland's tranquility was rudely shattered late in the eighth century by the arrival of the Vikings. These Norsemen preferred attacking Ireland's monasteries because they were usually defenseless and were therefore easily overrun. The monasteries also had treasuries that were filled with gold, silver, and precious gems and were well supplied with food such as corn, meat, and wine. But the assaults on the monasteries deprived the Irish of more than just possessions; the Vikings also removed the learning that Ireland was so noted for by killing or carrying away into slavery the monastic scholars.

Eventually the Vikings were largely driven out, but in 1169 Ireland faced an even mightier foe: the English. Armed with spears and light battle-axes, the Irish were no match for England's armor-clad horsemen and archers with longbows. The Irish fought stubbornly, but within a few years the English had conquered Ireland.

It was a curious type of conquest, however. Although the English remained dominant in running the country, they were actually being submerged into Irish society through intermarriage. Many English married and took Irish surnames, and soon it was impossible to tell the English from the native Irish. The English tried to address this problem in 1366 by enacting the Statutes of Kilkenny, which forbade English settlers to marry the Irish; speak their language; use their laws; support Irish poets, bards, or minstrels; wear Irish clothing; or adopt local customs.

It would remain an uneasy conquest for England because of the continual struggle by the Irish against British rule. Even centuries later, during the nineteenth century, the English poet and essayist Matthew Arnold brooded over "the Irish problem" in his essay *The Incompatibles:*

> England holds Ireland, say the Irish, by means of conquest and confiscation. But almost all countries have undergone conquest and confiscation. . . . After such proceedings, however, people go about their daily business, gradually things settle down and nobody talks about conquest and confiscation any more. But in Ireland . . . the conquest had to be again and again renewed. The angry memory of conquest and confiscation, the ardor for revolt against them, have continued therefore to irritate and inflame men's minds.[2]

Failed Rebellions

One of the numerous times that Ireland tried to throw off England's yoke was during the early twelfth century, when a young Scottish prince named Edward Bruce tried to reestablish Irish independence. His brother Robert had thrown the English out of Scotland, and Edward's goal was to help ensure Scottish independence by forcing England to divert its military to Ireland. The revolt fizzled, however, and Edward Bruce was killed. Ireland remained in Britain's grasp, although the English were unsuccessful in stamping out Irish culture.

But from time to time, England's political grip on Ireland very nearly slipped. In 1534 another uprising against British authority occurred when the Irish lords Gerald Óg Fitzgerald and his son "Silken Thomas" rebelled against the British. But this insurrection was also unsuccessful; Silken Thomas was executed for his trouble.

This failed rebellion made England's King Henry VIII realize that a radically new approach was needed to enforce British domination of Irish affairs. Henry knew he could not afford to recruit or equip a large army to occupy Ireland, which is what it would have taken to subdue the whole country. Thus, another method of control was needed.

*Ireland's chieftains, shown here in this woodcut, made re-
peated attempts to free their country from English rule.*

Henry Is Declared Ireland's King

Henry's first step in reasserting the British Crown's control
over Ireland came in 1537, when he declared himself the
supreme head of the Church of England, a title that applied
in Ireland as well as in England. This move severed all ties
between Henry and the church in Rome, and he hoped that
setting himself up as not only the political head of state but
also as the religious head would weaken the pope's influence
in Ireland.

But Henry went further. In 1541 the British Crown declared its ownership of all Irish lands. The king then granted
the land back to those Irish who were loyal to him. Henry VIII
also declared himself king of Ireland—instead of lord of Ireland, as his predecessors had done—meaning that Ireland was
now being directly ruled by Henry. The king further required
that the Irish lords receiving land learn English instead of
Gaelic and stop wearing distinctly Irish clothing in favor of
British-style clothing.

These actions represented a change from the previous
English philosophy that had produced the Statutes of
Kilkenny, under which the Irish were considered a unique

King Henry VIII of England attempted to weaken Irish cultural identity.

class of people. Now, the same laws that applied to the king's British subjects would apply to his Irish subjects as well. By confiscating Irish lands and then awarding them to Irish nobles who supported him, Henry was, in effect, buying their allegiance. And by making the grants contingent on the nobles' adoption of the English mode of dress and language, Henry was effectively attacking Irish culture from the top down.

Religious Struggle

Another tactic that Henry used to turn the Irish into loyal Eng-lishmen was to require them to renounce allegiance to the pope in favor of Anglicanism. Henry hoped that Anglicizing Irish religious practices would weaken Ireland's grip on the "old ways," which he believed the church at Rome represented.

When Henry died in 1547, his heir, Edward, continued his repressive policies toward the Irish. Under Edward, not only was the Church of England the official church of Ireland, but the Irish were also forbidden from celebrating the Catholic Mass. Edward even went so far as to order the destruction of holy relics, such as the staff that St. Patrick was supposed to have carried.

Edward died at age fifteen, and a period of instability followed. The king was succeeded by his devoutly Catholic half sister Mary Tudor, who restored the Catholic Church's dominance in Ireland. But just five years later Mary was followed to the British throne by another of Henry's daughters, Elizabeth, who reimposed Anglicanism.

All of these efforts to make the Irish more English failed. The old Gaelic ways that Henry and his successors sought to eliminate did not die easily. Although technically all of Ireland was subject to English rule, true English control was confined to the Pale, a strip along the eastern coast near Dublin approximately thirty miles wide and forty miles long. Furthermore, the English had to deal with a series of rebellions by various Irish nobles, including Shane O'Neill, Gerald Fitzgerald, and Hugh O'Neill.

The Flight of the Earls

The British policy of suppressing Catholicism was reinforced in 1607, when many Catholic nobles fled northern Ireland for Europe to avoid persecution after Hugh O'Neill's failed rebellion. The English king, James I, took their land and redistributed it to English and Scottish Protestant supporters. King James stipulated that those who received the land should also bring in Protestant tenants to cultivate the soil and build defenses. Altogether, several thousand Protestants moved into northern Ireland, altering the region forever and setting the stage for centuries of religious strife.

Ironically, the north had been the most Catholic part of Ireland before what became known as the Flight of the Earls occurred. England had tried "planting" settlers in Ireland before, but the Ulster Plantation was the first instance in which this strategy proved successful. The new settlers cleared the land, established towns, and in the process made the region their own.

However, since there were not enough Protestant settlers to completely populate the area, some Irish remained. Originally, the English plan was to segregate the Protestant colonists from the Irish Catholics, but the idea was never carried out. Gradually the Irish, forced by economic pressure, became tenants and laborers for the wealthy Protestant landlords. This created a tradition of bitterness between the two communities that would simmer for centuries.

The Ulster Plantation created a system under which Irish peasants would work the land for the landlord, who often remained at home in England. The tenant farmer had no rights and led an uncertain life as a result. For example, he could be evicted from land that his family had worked for generations if he had a bad harvest one season and could not pay the rent that the landlord demanded.

For their part, the Irish tenants could make life difficult for the absentee landlord. The Irish peasants tended to pack up and leave when faced with a bad harvest that would leave them unable to pay the rent. Peasants normally had few possessions, so it was easy for them to vacate their one-room cottages. Consequently, the absentee English landlord never knew if the peasants he thought were working his land were actually doing so. If he depended on the money he obtained in the form of rent and from the sale of crops, then the landlord faced financial reverses if it stopped abruptly.

Harsh Feelings

Aside from the hardship that could follow a bad harvest, the British measures to control Ireland affected the Irish peasants less than they did the Irish nobility. The English focused on keeping Ireland's lords and earls in line, on the theory that the rest of the population would follow. And from a practical standpoint, England's reach was not long enough to stretch into every Irish town and hamlet. What this meant, particularly as it pertained to religion, was that Irish peasants generally did things the traditional way, which included practicing Catholicism.

The Irish embraced Catholicism wholeheartedly and practiced their faith even in the face of hardship. As James Johnston, an eminent London physician once said, "In no country have I observed the people more zealous and sincere in the religious devotions than the Catholics of Ireland. If the chapel be full, you will see them on their knees around the doors exposed to the winds and rains."[3]

Yet the resentment between the Irish and the English periodically bubbled to the surface, resulting in open warfare. And

Oliver Plunket (1629–1681)

Considered in Ireland to be a hero on a par with St. Patrick, Oliver Plunket was born near Dublin into a leading Anglo-Irish family. At the age of sixteen he was sent to finish his education in Rome, and he was ordained a priest in 1654. In 1669 he became the leading Roman Catholic Church representative in Ireland.

Although sympathetic to the Irish Catholic nobility, Plunket continually urged them to make their peace with the British. When the British began a crackdown on Catholic clergy in 1673, however, he was forced to go into hiding. He was captured in 1678, was convicted in June 1681 on a trumped-up charge of inciting a rebellion in Ireland, and was executed by the British.

in war both sides used particularly brutal tactics. Determined to put down any rebellion, the English would burn villages, destroy crops and dwellings, and kill the inhabitants. Not to be outdone, the Irish would slaughter the English whenever the opportunity presented itself.

The result of all of this fighting was to transform what had once been a prosperous, green land into a cauldron of death and destruction. In the end, the Irish peasants suffered the most. In 1596 the English poet Edmund Spenser wrote about the unfortunate inhabitants of one Irish region:

Out of every corner of the woods and glens they came creeping forth upon their hands, for their legs could not bear them; they looked like anatomies of death; they spake like ghosts crying out of their graves; they did eat the dead carrions, happy where they could find them; yea, and one another soon after insomuch as the very carcasses they spared not to scrape out of their graves; and if they found a plot of watercresses or shamrocks, there they flocked as to feast for the time, yet not able long to continue there withal.[4]

England felt justified in using extreme measures for putting down Irish rebellions because keeping Ireland under English rule prevented what England feared most: an alliance between the Catholic countries of Ireland and Spain. At the time Spain was a powerful empire, and the English were afraid of being conquered by it. If the Catholics were to come to power in Ireland, went the theory, soon thereafter the Span-

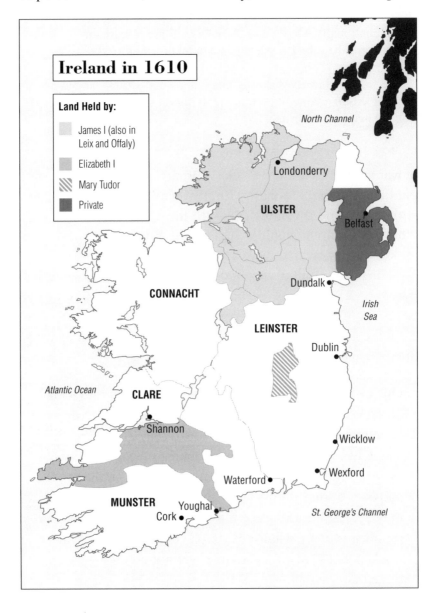

Ireland in 1610

Land Held by:

James I (also in Leix and Offaly)

Elizabeth I

Mary Tudor

Private

North Channel

Londonderry

ULSTER

Belfast

Dundalk

CONNACHT

Irish Sea

LEINSTER

Dublin

Atlantic Ocean

CLARE

Shannon

Wicklow

Wexford

Waterford

MUNSTER

Youghal

Cork

St. George's Channel

ish would be in a position to come sweeping down on England.

Repressive Laws

To prevent such an alliance, the English continued their attempt to assimilate the Irish into England's culture—in particular to make the country less Catholic. England tried to accomplish this through repressive laws designed to cripple Catholicism.

One of the first attempts came in 1560, when the Acts of Uniformity and Supremacy were passed. This made it mandatory to use the English prayer book in Ireland's churches. Then, in 1704, came the even harsher Penal Laws.

The activities forbidden by the Penal Laws were many and varied. Among other prohibitions, no Catholic could be a member of the Irish Parliament; buy or receive land from a Protestant; attend a university, be a teacher, or send his children to school abroad; hold a commission in the armed forces; or vote.

Discrimination against the Catholics touched virtually every facet of life. For example, if a Catholic owned a horse worth more than five pounds, any Protestant was entitled to purchase the animal for that same sum, regardless of whether its owner wished to sell.

Rebellion

It was only a matter of time before such measures would lead to rebellion. In 1641 the native Irish in Ulster rose up in what became known as the Protestant Massacre. The conflict was called this because during the fighting thousands of Protestant settlers were attacked and killed by Irish Catholics. Sometimes the murders were brutal, such as those at Portadown in County Armagh, where approximately one hundred Protestant men, women, and children were abducted from their homes and thrown from a bridge into the Bann River below. Those who struggled to shore were shot or had their skulls bashed in by the Irish. The uprising lasted until 1649. In that year England's ruler, Oliver Cromwell, landed in Ireland with an army to put down the rebellion.

British ruler Oliver Cromwell tried to stamp out Catholicism in Ireland.

Cromwell, like many of his predecessors, sought to enhance English control by converting most of the Irish to Protestantism. To accomplish this, Cromwell and his followers hunted down and imprisoned or exiled members of the Irish Catholic clergy. The English also seized the landholdings of many nobles living in southern Ireland. Even those Catholics who had not participated in the revolt were stripped of their lands and were herded into huge reservations.

Cromwell's goal was to force all Catholics into the province of Connacht, a sparsely inhabited region of lands too infertile for farming. Catholics who resisted faced a possible death sentence. Thus, Catholic landowners were said to have a choice of going "to Hell or Connacht."[5]

But Cromwell was only partially successful in his religious quest. He failed to win many converts, although through his actions he managed to impoverish many Irish Catholics. For example, in 1641 Irish Catholics had owned 59 percent of Ireland's land. That figure had dropped to 22 percent by 1660, after Cromwell had tried to stamp out Catholicism.

Cromwell died in 1658, but conditions for the Irish did not improve in the decades that followed. In fact, the poverty in which the Irish lived worsened dramatically during the eighteenth century, due in part to population growth. The population of Ireland rose from 2.5 million to 5 million between 1700 and 1800, so the lands available for Irish tenants to farm was increasingly subdivided into smaller and smaller parcels, until many families were eking out a meager existence on plots as small as two acres. Land became so scarce that many Protestant landlords could rent it out to the highest bidder and evict those who could not pay the higher rents. As a consequence, Ireland became home to a large class of landless beggars who wandered about the country in search of food and work.

Living conditions for those Irish who still had homes were predictably miserable. As one writer wrote about the country in the 1770s,

> The cottages of the Irish, which are called cabbins, are the most miserable looking hovels that can well be conceived. . . . The furniture of the cabbins is as bad as the architecture; in very many consisting only of a pot for boiling their potatoes, a bit of a table, and one or two broken stools; beds are not found universally, the family lying on straw.[6]

The Irish chafed under these conditions, but despite occasional uprisings, Ireland remained firmly in England's grasp. But the combination of the successful American Revolution against the British that ended in 1783 and the eruption of the French Revolution in 1789 lit yet another fire of rebellion in Ireland.

Reinvigorated Irish nationalism led to the formation of an organization called the Society of United Irishmen, founded in 1791 by a lawyer named Theobald Wolfe Tone. Although a Protestant, Tone was a Presbyterian—another group that had been largely pushed to the margins of Irish society. As its name suggested, the United Irishmen had as its goal a unification of the Protestant and Catholic communities to achieve Irish independence.

Under Tone's leadership the United Irishmen rose in revolt against the English in 1798. The revolt failed after only a few months, however, and Tone was captured in September of that year. He tried to cut his throat in prison but succeeded only in cutting his windpipe instead. Tone's wry observation was reportedly, "I find I am but a bad anatomist."[7] Tone lingered for eight days before dying.

A Union with Great Britain

In 1800 came another blow to Irish independence: The Irish Parliament voted to dissolve and join the British Isles and Scotland as part of the United Kingdom, letting the English government at Westminster make all decisions for the country. Under what was known as the Act of Union, Ireland was allotted just 100 members in the British House of Commons out of 658 members. Even if all of the Irish members voted as a bloc, they were greatly outnumbered.

The Act of Union was the brainchild of British prime minister William Pitt. He thought that uniting England and Ireland would benefit both countries. Great Britain was preparing to go to war with France, and the Act of Union would help garner Irish assistance in that conflict. Pitt also thought the act would encourage British investment in Ireland. Furthermore, Pitt saw the Act of Union helping Irish Protestants by changing their status from a minority in that country to a majority as part of Great Britain.

Another way that Pitt sought to assimilate Irish society into Great Britain was by article 5 of the Act of Union. This stated that the Protestant Church would offically become the church of Ireland. Thus, the church of just 5 percent of Ireland's population was established as the only church in Ireland.

Those Irish who wanted independence for their country protested that the Act of Union only passed because of massive efforts on the part of the British to corrupt the Irish legislators. Reportedly, over a million English pounds were used for direct bribes to Irish lawmakers to ensure approval of the bill. In addition, new titles of nobility were given to over two dozen Irish politicians, and many of those who already held titles were given higher ones.

The Irish did not willingly accept this union with Britain. In fact, unrest was so strong and frequent that many English mili-

Robert Emmet (1778–1803)

Another of the failed rebellions against British rule was led by Robert Emmet in 1803. Emmet was a former college student who had become affiliated withe the revolutionary group known as the United Irishmen.

In July 1803 Emmet led a small band of between 100 and 150 men in what was supposed to be an attack on Dublin Castle, the seat of the British government in Ireland. But the group was poorly organized and it took just a small group of British soldiers to disperse them. Emmet was subsequently caught, imprisoned, and hanged.

tary leaders considered Ireland to be not the soil of the United Kingdom but enemy territory. Yet many English Protestants also shared Pitt's belief that the status quo could not be maintained. Pitt had observed, "Ireland is like a ship on fire, it must either be extinguished or cut adrift."[8] Since letting Ireland leave the British Empire was not an option, the British had to extinguish the fires of independence—by uniting with it.

Daniel O'Connell

Although Irish nationalists vehemently opposed the union with Great Britain, they lacked a true leader to unify them and harness their anger. That changed when Daniel O'Connell arrived on the political stage. He was the Catholic son of a landlord in County Kerry. In 1793 Parliament had relaxed some of the restrictions against Catholics to try and defuse some of their rising anger. O'Connell had taken this opportunity to become a lawyer.

Known as "the Liberator," O'Connell was an excellent organizer and a gifted orator. He focused on two main objectives: complete repeal of laws restricting the rights of Catholics and the repeal of Ireland's union with Great Britain.

In 1823 O'Connell founded the Catholic Association, whose goal was to deliver the Catholic vote en masse to whichever candidate agreed to work on behalf of Catholics. To maximize membership, O'Connell set the association's dues at just a penny a month—which came to be known as the Catholic rent.

Using his often-hypnotic oratory, O'Connell held countless meetings on Irish hillsides attended by thousands of peasants. His message usually was that Ireland's Catholics would not be kept down forever: "The Catholic cause is on its majestic march; its progress is rapid and obvious. It is cheered in its advance and aided by all that is dignified and dispassionate. And its success is just as certain as the return of tomorrow's eve."[9]

In 1828 O'Connell ran for the British Parliament, even though he could not legally take a seat if elected. Still, there was nothing to stop him from running, and he won in a landslide. The British government, realizing that other Catholics would likely copy O'Connell's tactics, passed the Catholic Emancipation Act in 1829, removing all of the remaining restrictions on Catholics, including their exclusion from Great Britain's political process. O'Connell then took his seat in Parliament.

Daniel O'Connell addresses a gathering in County Meath. O'Connell worked to dissolve Ireland's union with Great Britain.

For twelve years O'Connell worked within Parliament, supporting leaders who promised to help the Irish. During this time, he steadfastly refused to sanction violence, once saying, "The winning of my country's freedom is not worth the shedding of a single drop of human blood."[10] Eventually, however, O'Connell lost hope that Irish interests could be served by remaining a part of Great Britain, and in 1841 he began a movement called the Repeal Association, whose stated goal was repeal of the Act of Union. O'Connell used the same tactics as before: mass rallies to pressure the government. But the British had no intention of dissolving the union with Ireland. A few hours before the last and biggest rally was to be held, the English government banned the demonstration.

O'Connell was in a dilemma. He knew that canceling the meeting would be unpopular with his supporters, yet he knew that a clash was likely if the British government's troops confronted the demonstrators. O'Connell chose to cancel the gathering, and the decision ended his political power. Many Irish thought he had simply lost his nerve, and the lesson that many Irish took from the affair was that violence would be needed to achieve independence.

Nationalists like O'Connell and Tone had kept glowing the embers of the yearning for Irish independence. In the decades to come, those embers would burst into full flame.

Battles for Independence 2

For a time, the issue of nationalism receded into the background of Irish consciousness. For many Irish, the overwhelming concern was simply in finding enough to eat.

The Great Famine

Ireland, one of the most densely populated countries in Europe, saw its troubles intensify in 1845 when a mysterious blight began attacking the potato crop and depriving the Irish peasant of a primary food source. During the years of what came to be known as the Potato Famine, an estimated 1.5 million people died of starvation and attendant diseases. Another 1 million people immigrated to North America (mainly the United States) aboard overcrowded ships. Conditions for the immigrants were so unsanitary and substandard that the vessels came to be known as coffin ships because of the many people who died before they reached port. Still, many chose to take their chances. As a result, the population of Ireland dropped to 6.2 million by 1851 from a high of around 8 million in 1847.

The famine's victims were mainly the Irish tenant farmers who depended on the potato for their sustenance, a fact that magnified the resentment that the native Irish held for the English landowners. If potatoes were not available for the landlord, he merely ate something else since other crops, such as wheat, were unaffected by the blight.

But wheat was too expensive for most tenant farmers to afford; without potatoes, Irish tenants could—and often did—die. Some landlords provided help for their tenants during the famine by giving them food and other necessities, but others simply ignored their tenants and let them starve.

During the Potato Famine, Irish tenant farmers who were unable to pay their rent were often evicted from their homes.

The British government took little direct action to address the problem. Basing its policies on the theory that market forces must be allowed free rein and that a massive relief effort would disrupt Ireland's economy, the government largely left the Irish to fend for themselves. Those Irish who survived and did not emigrate nurtured a burning hatred for their English masters.

In addition to depriving the Irish of their primary food source, the Potato Famine further impoverished an already poor people since potatoes were also a cash crop. Without potatoes, the Irish tenant farmer often had no way to pay his English landlord the rent he owed. Consequently, many Irish were evicted from their homes. Between the evictions and the people who had fled to America, Ireland became a country of abandoned dwellings and farms.

The Famine's Legacy

The Potato Famine had a searing effect on the Irish for decades. As Father John A. O'Brien would one day note,

> The Famine had the catastrophic proportions of a continuing earthquake that shook the inhabitants from their ancient moorings in the green island and set them scurrying in headlong haste to America, Canada, Australia, Great Britain, New Zealand, and all the countries of the world. Its terror and horror have gnawed their way into the inner marrow of the race's memory and would seem to have left upon the Gaelic soul a wound so deep that even the passage of a century has failed to heal it.[11]

The graphic evidence that the English did not care about the people of Ireland was not lost on the Irish Republican Brotherhood, an organization founded in 1858. Brotherhood members called themselves Fenians after a group of ancient Irish warriors. Moreover, the Irish Republican Brotherhood's founders believed that physical force was the only way to win independence from

Irish emigrants camp at the dockside in Cork while waiting for a ship to take them to America.

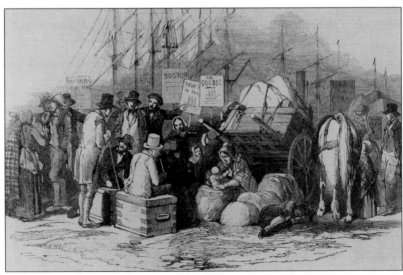

England. The Fenians' message appealed to all of the radical elements in both Irish politics and Irish society.

Home Rule

Others were more inclined to use political means to achieve at least some measure of autonomy for Ireland. Isaac Butt, a scholar and lawyer who had represented several leaders of the Irish Republican Brotherhood who had run afoul of British authorities, was one such individual. In 1870 Butt formed the Home Government Association (HGA).

The HGA and its successor organization, the Home Rule League (HRL) had one goal: to form an Irish parliament. Butt and his fellow HGA members contended that the British government neglected Ireland's affairs, and that an Irish parliament would do a better job of managing the country. "I have long since had the conviction forced upon me," said Butt, "that it is equally essential to the safety of England and to the happiness and tranquility of Ireland that the right of self-government should be restored to this country."[12] The campaign for Irish self-government became known as home rule.

In his efforts to achieve home rule, Butt was aided by another Irish member of Parliament, Charles Stewart Parnell. Despite the efforts of Butt and Parnell, however, the British Parliament continued to drag its feet on the issue. To pressure Parliament, Parnell and other home rule advocates initiated a policy of obstruction in the legislative body. By using administrative and parliamentary maneuvers to disrupt the routine business of government, such as approving budgets, home rule advocates were able to lend urgency to the issue.

The Land League

Parnell was a fiery orator, and he replaced Butt as the leader of the home-rule movement. Meanwhile, he also sought to have the British government address a specific Irish grievance: the fact that so much Irish land was actually owned—illegitimately, he believed—by English landlords. In 1879 Parnell became president of the Land League, an organization founded that

Charles Stewart Parnell addresses members of the Irish Land League, a group that agitated for the return of the land to Irish ownership.

same year by a Fenian named Michael Davitt and dedicated to returning Ireland's land to Irish ownership. Parnell's passionate speeches in favor of land reform and his membership in the HRL meant that home rule and Irish ownership of Ireland's lands became the dominant political issues of the day.

The agitation and unrest fomented by Parnell and the Land League finally motivated Britain's prime minister, William Gladstone, to introduce the Land Act of 1881. This measure was based on the principle of the three F's: fixity of tenure (so that tenant farmers could not suddenly be evicted), fair rents, and free sale. Special land courts were established with the power to set rents for fifteen years so that a landlord could not suddenly raise it.

This land reform measure, however, fell far short of the Land League's demand for the complete return of all lands to Irish ownership. The unrest in Ireland continued; a British official reported to the cabinet at this time that "the state of the country is undoubtedly most serious."[13]

In response to the continued agitation, Gladstone had the Land League's leaders, including Parnell, arrested and imprisoned in October 1881. However, this move did not end the unrest but rather escalated it. In addition, other Land League members urged tenant farmers to withhold rents until their grievances had been addressed. The British government responded by suppressing the Land League, which only exacerbated the conflict.

Parnell was released six months later with the understanding that he would use his influence to help calm the situation in Ireland. In exchange, the British Parliament undertook the first steps to return the land to the people of Ireland. Parnell had won the land-reform battle.

The Downfall of Parnell

With land reform accomplished, Parnell was a hero to the Irish people. He then turned his attention to home rule. Victory seemed possible when, in 1886, Gladstone introduced into Parliament a bill calling for home rule for Ireland. When the bill lost by just thirty votes, it seemed very possible that upon reintroduction the bill would garner the necessary votes. At long last, Ireland seemed about to gain a measure of independence.

But then something totally unexpected happened. In November 1890 William Henry O'Shea, a former member of Parnell's political party, sued his wife, Kitty, for divorce, alleging that she was having an affair with Parnell. When Parnell made no effort to contest it, the allegation was generally assumed to be true.

Irish regard for Parnell was generally undiminished, but the English were aghast at his behavior. Gladstone knew that to align himself with an admitted adulterer would be political suicide, and so he distanced himself from both Parnell and his home-rule movement.

Now on the defensive, whereas he had once been treated almost like a deity by Irish voters, Parnell tried desperately to recover his lost political power. But no amount of campaigning could bring back his favorable mystique. While on a grueling speaking tour in early October, his health gave out. On October 6, 1891, Charles Stewart Parnell died at the age of forty-five.

Sinn Féin

With the death of Parnell, all of the various factions that he had held together in the home rule movement went their separate ways. Numerous competing organizations formed, such as the Gaelic Athletic Association and the Gaelic League. Both were supposedly nonpolitical groups, yet as their titles suggested, both championed ancient Ireland and its traditions, so both were nationalistic in a very real sense. Another organization that formed in 1908 and did not hide the fact that it was extremely political was Sinn Féin (We Ourselves). This group's goal was simple and direct: reestablishing the independence of Ireland.

Maneuvering for Home Rule

Nearly twenty years after the fact, memories of the Parnell scandal had faded, and to many, it looked as if Sinn Féin's goal was within reach. The election of 1910 put the Irish home rule advocates firmly in a position of power in the British Parliament. The Liberals, who generally supported home rule, had won control of the English government by a narrow margin. The Conservatives, who generally opposed home rule, were strong enough that the Liberals needed the support of other political parties to pass legislation in the British House of Commons. Since the home rule advocates were the most powerful group available with which to

Violent protests in Ireland eventually motivated Britain's Parliament to pass a home rule bill.

form an alliance, a tacit deal for support was struck between the Liberals and the proponents of home rule.

Giving further hope to the Irish was the fact that the House of Lords, the highly conservative second branch of the British legislature, was only in a position to delay home rule. The members of the House of Lords might well disapprove of a home rule bill, but the most they could do was delay its implementation by two years.

The Ulster Reaction

It seemed inevitable, therefore, that a home rule bill would pass the British Parliament. But not all of Ireland was happy about that fact. In particular, the residents of six northern counties—Armagh, Cavan, Donegal, Derry, Fermanagh, and Tyrone—were horrified at the prospect of home rule. Ever since the days of the Ulster Plantation, this region had been a stronghold of English Protestants. Because Ireland as a whole was overwhelmingly Catholic, these residents viewed home rule as tantamount to

being ruled by the pope. The Ulster Protestants were determined
to prevent that. Many of them joined an organization called the
Orange, or the Orangemen, whose goal was to prevent home rule.

Carson Rallies the Unionists

In 1910 the anti–home rule Irish Unionist Party in Ulster chose
Edward Carson as its leader. Carson was a Dublin-born lawyer,
as spellbinding in a courtroom as he was on the campaign
stump. Although he was not as vehemently anti-Catholic as
some other Ulster Protestant politicians, Carson was convinced
that Ireland's welfare was best served by keeping the country
within the British Empire.

In 1911 Carson, alarmed by the prospect of home rule,
said, "We must be prepared, in the event of a Home Rule Bill
passing, with such measures as will carry on for ourselves the
government of those districts of which we have control."[14]
This was an audacious comment, suggesting that if home rule
passed, the Unionists would ignore it and set up their own
government.

Protestants in Ulster showed that Carson's words were no
idle threat by holding a huge pro-union rally in September 1912,
at which 218,000 Orangemen signed their names—some liter-
ally using their own blood—to an anti–home rule petition.

Edward Carson (1854–1935)

Often considered the architect of Northern Ireland, early in his
career Edward Carson was a lawyer, and he won many cases on
behalf of absentee British landlords against tenant farmers. In
1910 Carson's extreme distaste for Irish independence and home
rule drove him to take control of the union movement in Ulster.

Carson threatened armed rebellion if home rule was
granted, and he founded the Ulster Volunteers, a quasi-military
group, to carry forth on this threat. The British wilted before
his fervent opposition and, in 1920, made Ulster a separate
country.

Home Rule

That which Carson was so afraid of—a home rule bill—was introduced into the House of Commons in April 1912. The legislation was extremely limited in scope. There would be an Irish parliament, but the British would continue to control defense, relations with England, the police, and even revenue.

Some nationalists liked the new arrangement, seeing it as just a first step that would eventually lead to total independence. But Sinn Féin condemned it, calling it too little. "If this is liberty the lexicographers [dictionary authors] have deceived us,"[15] said Arthur Griffith, one of the group's founders.

As expected, the Unionists hated the measure. But despite their opposition, the bill passed the House of Commons in January 1913. The House of Lords quickly rejected it, but everyone knew that, at most, the lords' rejection could only delay home rule for two years. In Ireland, pro- and anti-Unionists had two years to prepare for the inevitability of home rule.

Those preparations suggested that the response to home rule by its opponents would be violent. In Ulster a group called the Ulster Volunteer Force began arming itself. The pro–home rule forces countered with the creation of the Irish Volunteers. Another group that formed was the Citizen Army, which was supposedly defending the rights of workers in southern Ireland but was also pro–home rule. Finally, there was the Irish Republican Brotherhood, which was the most extreme of the nationalist militias. The threat of violence escalated in April 1914, when the Ulster Volunteers bought 35,000 rifles and 3 million rounds of ammunition from Germany and drilled openly with the weapons.

The Catholic Church came out steadfastly against violence. But the church's position mattered little to the Irish nationalists, who had convinced themselves that the church, and even the pope, did not understand the issues. Thus, the nationalists reasoned that since the church was laboring under a mistaken impression, then its preachings against violence were not binding. Surely, the nationalists argued, if church leaders understood

Demonstrators and police battle each other during a home rule riot.

what was at stake, then they would at the very least look the other way and not condemn the use of force. In the end, even though most Irish Catholics were outwardly devout—Mass attendance among Irish Catholics had been estimated at approximately 90 percent in 1900—church opposition ultimately did little to avert violence.

England's Danger Is Ireland's Opportunity

With all of these paramilitary forces at large, Ireland resembled an armed camp. Violence, however, broke out not in Ireland but hundreds of miles away as Germany invaded Belgium and then France, touching off the conflict that came to be known as World War I.

When war broke out in Europe in August 1914, consideration of the home-rule question was suspended. Both Carson and John Redmond, leader of the pro–home rule the Irish National Party, agreed to support England in its war efforts since a mutual defense pact obligated England to support France against Germany. A compromise between Unionists and home rule advocates was reached, under which home rule for Ireland was passed into law but then suspended until the cessation of hostilities between England and Germany.

This compromise suited Carson, but to some of Redmond's followers, this delay represented an outright betrayal of their cause. A popular ditty sprang up that illustrated how deeply some Irish resented fighting for England when home rule was being denied them: "Full steam ahead, John Redmond said, that everything was well chum; Home Rule will come when we are dead and buried out in Belgium."[16]

Some historians believe that in setting aside home rule in this way Carson and Redmond squandered an opportunity to resolve the home-rule question and avoid violence. England, preoccupied with the war, needed Ireland's support and perhaps, some say, could have been persuaded to settle the matter in a way acceptable to both sides. But with the agreement to ignore the whole issue of Ireland's status until Germany was defeated, Britain had no reason to make settling the matter a priority. By the time home rule once again became paramount, violence had stained the green of Ireland blood red.

John Redmond (1856–1918)

The leader of the Irish National Party from 1900 to 1918, Redmond was a loyal supporter of famous Irish nationalist leader Charles Stewart Parnell. Upon Parnell's fall from grace, Redmond eventually became leader of the Nationalist movement. In 1914 Redmond threw his political support to the Liberal Party, which was battling the Conservative Party for control of the British government. In return, the Liberals pushed through a home rule bill for Ireland. But the outbreak of World War I suspended enactment of the measure. When Redmond promised Irish support of Britain during the war, it strengthened the radical Irish nationalists. They staged the Easter Rising of 1916, which Redmond initially denounced as a German plot—showing how removed he was from the Irish independence movement. Thereafter, Redmond lost both power and popularity, and he died in 1918 without seeing home rule enacted.

The Easter Rising

One group of Irishmen saw an opportunity in World War I and decided to seize it. They were the radical Irish Republican Brotherhood (IRB), who believed, as did their political partners in Sinn Féin, that it was Britain, not Ireland, that had a quarrel with Germany. They also believed that with England preoccupied by war with Germany, armed rebellion could achieve what political maneuvering had failed to gain. With the IRB inclined to fight, Ireland was ready to explode.

The explosion, when it came, was touched off by a young poet-schoolteacher named Patrick Pearse. Pearse was obsessed with the idea of the blood sacrifice: Blood being shed in battle in pursuit of a heroic objective was well spent. For him, there could be no higher goal than the liberation of Ireland.

Pearse talked and wrote in the blood-and-thunder rhetoric of an ancient warrior. Early in 1916, at a funeral oration, Pearse said, "We must not flinch when we are passing through that uproar [war]; we must not faint at the sight of blood."[17]

Pearse's wish for military action was soon fulfilled. Expecting help from Germany in the form of arms and advisers, the IRB set Easter Monday 1916 as the day the armed rebellion would begin. Even before the rebellion began, though, plans went awry. A German supply ship, the *Aud,* carrying twenty thousand rifles, was intercepted by British authorities off the Irish coast. Sir Roger Casement, who had arranged the arms shipment, tried to stop the uprising once he discovered that the guns had been captured. But when he landed on Irish soil he was arrested by British authorities, who had learned he was coming from information obtained during the interception of the arms shipment.

Several other revolt leaders, including James Connolly, also knew that the rebellion was doomed to failure and even told some would-be rebel supporters that their chances of success were nonexistent. The chief of staff of the IRB even sent out orders canceling the revolt. Now it was obvious that the rebellion was doomed to failure, but Pearse and his supporters, still locked into the image of the blood sacrifice, decided to proceed anyway.

Accordingly, on Easter Monday, April 24, 1916, approximately sixteen hundred Irish insurgents armed with rifles, sledgehammers, pikes, and homemade bombs took over several buildings in the middle of Dublin. From the steps of the general post office, Pearse read a proclamation declaring the establishment of an Irish republic, with himself as president. Then the poorly armed and ill-trained rebels withdrew into their buildings and waited for the British response.

Despite Casement's arrest, the British authorities were still taken by surprise by the uprising. But once they recovered, they attacked the rebels with fury, pouring thousands of soldiers into Dublin and shelling the occupied buildings.

By the second day British government forces were clearly gaining the upper hand. On Saturday, April 29, Pearse, who never fired a shot during the uprising, eventually surrendered with the other rebels when he personally witnessed the deaths

English soldiers and Irish civilians shoot at each other during the Easter Rising in Dublin.

of three civilians and decided to quit the fight rather than have any more civilians die. There were isolated instances of revolt elsewhere in Ireland, but most of the country remained peaceful. Approximately 1,351 rebels, soldiers, police, and civilians were killed or wounded in the ill-fated affair. Pearse had gotten his blood sacrifice.

The initial Irish reaction to the insurrection was negative. Thanks to the rebels' actions, life in Dublin had been disrupted. The trains were not running into parts of the city, many shops and pubs had been closed, and one of the few bakeries still open in town was located in the battle zone, so many people needing bread had to dodge rifle fire to get to it.

In addition, many Irish viewed the insurrection as an act of treason. Many thousands of Ireland's male citizens were serving in the British armed forces, and it was felt that if the rebels wanted to fight, they should join the other Irish on the front lines. The Catholic Church also condemned the revolt. As the defeated rebels were being taken to prison, crowds of people in Dublin booed them and threw rotten eggs and vegetables at them.

But Irish public opinion swung around in favor of the rebels as the British government began executing them. Between May 3 and May 12, fifteen of the leaders, including Pearse, were taken before firing squads, despite the warning from the influential Irish playwright George Bernard Shaw that the British were "canonizing their prisoners."[18] In particular, sympathy was aroused for the rebels when James Connolly, wounded so badly that he was unable to stand, was carried to the execution grounds on a stretcher and was shot while sitting in a chair.

By the time public outrage brought an end to the executions, late in May, the insurrection's leaders had become martyrs for the cause of Irish freedom and the populace was inflamed with nationalist sentiment. Sinn Féin became more powerful, and a new generation took over Ireland's independence movement. Men such as Eamon De Valera and Michael Collins would lead Ireland on the bloody path to which it was now irrevocably committed.

Birth of Two Nations 3

The main casualty of the ill-fated Easter Rising and the subsequent executions was any hope for a peaceful, parliamentary move toward Irish independence. In the months that followed, many Irish men and women who had been content to wait for the end of World War I before pressing for home rule became violent revolutionaries, flocking to the Sinn Féin banner. No longer was armed rebellion something favored by the few: Now thousands of Irish believed that only violence would bring them freedom.

Negotiations Bring Failure

The Easter Rising convinced the British government that it could not afford to wait until the end of the war with Germany to deal with Ireland. Thus, it entrusted David Lloyd George, a prominent member of the Liberal Party, with the task of solving what was known as the Irish Question.

Britain's David Lloyd George negotiated home rule for Ireland.

For almost two years, beginning in May 1916, Lloyd George held negotiations between the Unionists and the nationalists, trying to find common ground between the two sides. Eventually, these negotiations proved fruitless. However, they did further the notion of partition—meaning that the Ulster counties with strong English loyalties would be removed from the rest of Ireland and allowed to remain as part of the British Empire when home rule came to the remainder of the country. This idea gained so much legitimacy during this time that it became almost an article of faith in Irish politics. The bone of contention was that the unionists thought that the partition would be permanent, and the nationalists thought it was to be temporary.

The Radical Irish

Besides the execution of the Easter Rising leaders, the other event that propelled people into Sinn Féin and radicalized them was the announcement in April 1918 that the British government was considering imposing military conscription in Ireland. This meant that Irish males would have to serve in the British army and fight in World War I, no matter what their political views. Thousands of Irish now joined or pledged allegiance to Sinn Féin, convinced that only an Irish government should be able to order them to put their lives at risk. In addition, many Irish were genuinely opposed to serving the same nation that had executed the leaders of the Easter rebellion. Even the Catholic Church, which had long been neutral on the issue of Irish nationalism, denounced the conscription measure. The entire Irish delegation withdrew from the British Parliament in protest.

Ultimately, no Irishmen were forced into British uniforms, but that was beside the point. Just the fact that the British claimed the power to conscript them had turned many Irish into fire-breathing patriots. Before his execution for his part in the Easter Rising, Roger Casement had summed up what many Irish were feeling: "Ireland has no blood to give to any land or any cause, save Ireland."[19]

The shedding of blood was becoming ever more likely. The leader of the Sinn Féin party was now a fervent nationalist named Eamon De Valera, who had been a commandant in the Easter Rising and who had narrowly escaped facing a firing squad because he had been born in America. By that time

Arthur Griffith

The founder and first leader of Sinn Féin, Arthur Griffith was a journalist and a fierce nationalist. Griffith thought that some monarchical form of government would be necessary once Ireland gained its independence if the Irish did not want to lose the loyalty of the pro-British northern part of the country. Thus, he favored a dual monarchy system: a king for England and one with limited powers for Ireland.

Griffith was not a violent revolutionary, but when he concluded that only violence would bring results, he turned over the reins of Sinn Féin to Eamon De Valera. In 1921 Griffith was elected the first president of the Dáil of the Irish Free State after it became part of the British Commonwealth, but he died shortly afterward of exhaustion brought about by overwork.

Arthur Griffith (seated, fourth from left) with other members of Sinn Féin's Standing Committee.

the United States had entered the war against Germany, so the British, aware that the Irish wielded considerable political clout in the United States, commuted the sentences of De Valera and others. Later on, in June 1917, De Valera was released by Lloyd George, who had become the British prime minister, as part of a general amnesty toward all Irish political prisoners.

Another leader of Sinn Féin was Michael Collins, who was the director of organization. Efficient and ruthless, he had none of De Valera's political subtlety. Collins was apt to rush ahead and strike out whereas De Valera was more cunning and cautious. Collins prepared for guerrilla warfare with the British, convinced that Ireland was heading in that direction.

Recognizing that the threat of violence was growing, the British tried desperately to control the situation in Ireland. In May 1918 they jailed De Valera, proclaimed Sinn Féin illegal, and banned public meetings.

But these moves meant little. In the general election of December 14, 1918, barely a month after the end of World War I, the Irish populace showed how radical it had become. Sinn Féin candidates won a majority of the Irish seats in the British Parliament.

Then Sinn Féin added fuel to the fire. Rather than take their seats, the Sinn Féin members of Parliament traveled not to London but to Dublin instead, and on January 21, 1919, they proclaimed themselves to be the Dáil Éireann—the national assembly of the Republic of Ireland. In April, Eamon De Valera, who had escaped from jail in Great Britain in February, was elected president of the assembly.

The British could not allow this challenge to their authority to stand. A rival government in Ireland could give orders countermanding theirs, could order the people to perform anti-British acts, and in general could cause havoc and confusion. Still, there were attempts to avoid all-out war. During the summer of 1919, negotiations in the United States took place between De Valera, as Ireland's head of state, and representatives of the British government. These, however, proved futile in resolving the crisis in Ireland.

With the failure of diplomacy, isolated clashes began occurring in the fall of 1919 between the guerrilla army of the Irish republic—known as the Irish Republican Army (IRA)—and the British police forces, known as the Royal Irish Constabulary (RIC). By the middle of 1920 the attacks by the IRA had become more systematic and organized and amounted to steady warfare between the Irish and the British.

The Troubles

What is often referred to in Ireland as "the troubles" was actually a violent and often savage guerrilla war between Irish nationalists and British government forces. Lloyd George and his allies in the British government had only a slim majority in Parliament, and they did not want to admit that under their aegis a shooting war had developed in Ireland. They insisted instead that the conflict was a minor one that could be handled by the RIC and that it was not necessary to send in British troops.

The IRA took advantage of the fact that it did not have to face the might of the British army. The group also fought a kind of war for which the British were totally unprepared. IRA members wore civilian clothing rather than uniforms, and they appeared to be just ordinary citizens on the street—until they unleashed a vicious attack on the RIC. These innocent-looking citizen-soldiers became known as the flying columns of the IRA—groups of men who wore no uniform, lived on the move, and constantly carried weapons. They operated mainly in their local towns, and because they were known to the townspeople, they enjoyed broad public support and sympathy.

The result was that the IRA enjoyed great success against the RIC. In response, the British raised two new forces in England and sent them to Ireland. One was the Black and Tans, so named because of the color of their uniforms; the other was the Auxiliaries.

In the fighting that ensued, each force engaged in extraordinarily brutal tactics. For example, in one incident in which the Black and Tans captured and then killed six IRA members near the city of Cork, three of the victims were tortured and mutilated before they were killed. One had his heart cut out, one had his nose cut off, and another had his tongue cut out. The IRA employed equally grisly methods of killing: In one incident they

Members of the Black and Tans search a suspected Irish rebel at gunpoint.

captured a judge and then buried him up to his neck on a beach at low tide. He had no choice but to watch the water advance toward him before he drowned.

The war claimed many lives among noncombatants as well. The IRA executed civilians suspected of leaking information to the enemy; the British did the same with those they suspected of traitorous activities. Many people were caught in the middle, targeted by one or the other group as being too friendly with the other side. Particularly worrisome to civilians were the hours of curfew—typically after ten o'clock at night. After that hour civilians were confined to their homes. Yet they never knew when the British authorities would show up at their door to search their homes for suspected terrorists or arrest or even murder members of their families without provocation.

Perhaps the worst incident of all occurred on November 21, 1920—known as Bloody Sunday. During the morning the IRA broke into homes and killed fourteen British undercover agents, sometimes right in front of their families. That afternoon, a detachment of Black and Tans looking for the IRA gunmen shot indiscriminately into a crowd at a soccer stadium, killing twelve men and women and wounding sixty others.

Northern Ireland Comes into Being

Meanwhile, the six northern counties that had remained loyal to England suffered from their own level of violence. This took the form of riots by Protestants against Catholics, who often wanted only to be left alone but who were nonetheless victimized. Catholics were attacked in the streets and in their neighborhoods.

Riots first broke out in Belfast in the summer of 1920, but eventually they spread to other parts of Ulster over the next twelve months. Edward Carson's pro-Unionist forces were the chief instigators of the attacks, although Catholics and Protestants both suffered from the violence. Between July 1920 and June 1922, an estimated 267 Catholics and 185 Protestants were killed in the fighting.

The British government, proving incapable of protecting its Catholic subjects in Ulster, nonetheless decided that the only way to deal with the crisis in what Lloyd George referred to as "that beautiful, sad bitch of a country,"[20] was to divide it. By doing this, the British believed they would be establishing a Protestant nation much like their own—one whose citizens

William Butler Yeats (1865–1939)

Widely acknowledged as one of the greatest Irish poets, William Butler Yeats was originally uninterested in Irish politics. As a young man Yeats lived in London, and it was not until he traveled to Dublin and met the Irish freedom fighter Maud Gonne, with whom he fell madly in love, that he became involved in Irish nationalism. Following the Easter Rising in 1916, Yeats wrote a poem, "Easter 1916," which contained the now-famous line, "A terrible beauty is born."

Yeats was one of the founders of the famous Abbey Theatre in Dublin, which he helped develop into one of the leading theaters in the world and the center of the literary movement known as the Irish Renaissance. Yeats won the Nobel Prize for literature in 1923.

were loyal to the Crown and in whose interests they could intercede if necessary. Partition would also put the Protestant majority permanently in charge and quell Protestant fears of being subjugated by a Catholic majority.

Accordingly, the British government divided Ireland in two in December 1920. The six Ulster counties (Antrim, Armagh, Down, Fermanagh, Derry, and Tyrone) became the country of Northern Ireland, with its own parliament; the rest of the country was known as southern Ireland, or simply Ireland. It also had its own parliament. If both parliaments ever desired it, they could reunite into one country. The border between both countries was loosely drawn.

As was true virtually every time the British made a decision regarding Ireland, this one pleased nobody. The Ulster Unionists had never wanted partition, wanting instead to simply be, along with all the Irish, good subjects of the British Crown. But they realized that the partition, in which Protestants would outnumber Catholics two to one in Northern Ireland, was the best deal they were likely to get. The alternative was a unified, independent Ireland, which they vehemently opposed.

The Irish nationalists, for their part, were horrified at the idea of partition as well and vowed to fight it. But they were increasingly aware that the military situation in the country was becoming a stalemate: They could keep fighting, but they lacked the strength to force the British out of Ireland. Thus, support began to build for a peace treaty and a political solution.

What is clear is that the British never expected the partition of Ireland to be permanent. The agreement that split the country also called for the creation of the Boundary Commission, which was supposed to adjust the border between Ireland and Northern Ireland in accordance with the wishes of the inhabitants. Since two of the six counties that constituted Northern Ireland had Catholic majorities (Tyrone and Fermanagh), it was expected that they would eventually ask to be moved back into Ireland. That would leave the Ulster Unionists with a mere four-county nation, which was not considered to be economically viable.

King George Calls for Peace

Partition, therefore, failed to stop "the troubles." But support for a political solution to the seemingly stalemated war between Britain and Irish rebels increased dramatically on June 22, 1921, when the British king George V appeared at the opening of the Northern Ireland Parliament in Belfast.

At the opening-day ceremony the king, who had been deeply troubled by the events in Ireland, discarded his prepared speech and delivered an emotional plea from the heart, saying, "I appeal to all Irishmen to pause, to stretch out the hand of forbearance, and conciliation, and to join in making for the land which they love a new era of peace, contentment, and goodwill."[21]

The king's call to resolve the conflict yielded positive results in both the north and the south. All sides in the war understood that he was making a gesture of peace on behalf of the British government. The British had been under severe pressure both from home and abroad to end the war. Moreover, the Irish rebels had their own reason to agree to negotiate. Michael Collins had urgently warned De Valera that the IRA was on the verge of defeat—a fact of which the British were unaware.

Two days after the king's speech, Lloyd George invited the warring factions to a peace conference. On July 10 a truce was arranged between both sides, and the search for a permanent settlement began.

The negotiations dragged on for five months. There were actually two separate sets of negotiations, one in July 1921 with De Valera attending, and one that began in October 1921, with Collins and Arthur Griffith as the leaders. De Valera chose to remain out of the second round of negotiations. Why he did so is a matter of debate. De Valera simply said that it would be better if he remained in Ireland during this difficult time. Some historians, however, claim that De Valera knew that the negotiations would result in a treaty unfavorable for the Irish, and he wished to distance himself from it.

The British had two unyielding demands during the negotiations: that any free Irish state remain part of the British

King George V of England inspects an honor guard prior to opening Northern Ireland's Parliament in June 1921.

Commonwealth, and that Northern Ireland should not be forced to join a free Irish state.

On December 6, 1921, Britain and Ireland reached an agreement. The treaty called for the establishment in one year of the Irish Free State, which would have the same status as Canada—that is, a dominion of the British Crown. The English were allowed to keep naval bases at certain Irish ports and also remained responsible for coastal defense. The Irish would also have to take an oath of allegiance to the British Crown.

The British had warned the Irish delegation that if its members refused to sign the treaty the war would resume, with martial law being imposed. Military tribunals would replace civil courts, newspapers would be muzzled, and other civil liberties would be restricted. In addition, one hundred thousand British troops would be sent to Ireland.

With Collins realizing that the IRA could not survive another war with Great Britain, the Irish delegates signed the treaty. Some harbored no illusions about how unpopular the partition of the island, the oath of allegiance to the British king, and the substitution of dominion status for the long-dreamed-of republic would be with their countrymen. Collins, in particular, knew that he would be blamed for committing to the treaty. "I am signing my own death warrant,"[22] he said.

Dissension over the Treaty

It seemed as if the reason for conflict was over, but Irish politics proved more complicated than that. The Dáil split into two factions: One group endorsed the treaty as the best deal that could be gotten, but the other side condemned it, claiming that the delegates had no right to sign it, that any treaty with an oath of allegiance to the English king was unacceptable, and that a better deal could have been negotiated. A great debate ensued throughout Ireland, dividing the populace over the pros and cons of the treaty; even friends, such as De Valera and Collins, were divided over the issue.

On January 7, 1922, the Dáil voted sixty-four to fifty-seven to accept the treaty. De Valera immediately resigned the Irish presidency, and Griffith, one of the signers of the treaty, took his place.

On January 14 a provisional government, with Collins as chairman, came to power, but the division over the treaty refused to mend. De Valera and his followers continued their campaign against the treaty. The IRA was also split into pro and con factions. Meanwhile, British forces were evacuating the country, and it was often hard to determine if the barracks and other military facilities they left behind were being occupied by national or free-state forces (pro-treaty) or irregulars (anti-treaty).

An election was held in June 1922 to select deputies for the new Dáil. The election turned out to be a referendum on the treaty, and by a resounding 486,419 votes to 133,864, pro-treaty candidates defeated anti-treaty candidates. When De Valera and his anti-treaty followers refused to accept the results, civil war engulfed Ireland.

Civil War

The event that touched off the Irish Civil War was, ironically, the killing of a British general early in July 1922. In April 1922, irregulars had occupied a building complex known as the Four Courts, which served as the Dublin headquarters of the Irish judiciary. Collins had responded to the takeover cautiously, but when the irregulars killed Sir Henry Wilson, the British military adviser to Northern Ireland, Collins felt the rebels were becoming too bold and attacked those holed up in the Four Courts with artillery borrowed from the British. The irregulars surrendered, but open warfare between the irregulars and the new Irish government had begun.

The Irish Civil War was as bloody and savage as the previous war against England had been. Both sides in the conflict knew how to use terror tactics. Furthermore, the Irish were just as willing to use violence against one another as they had been to use it against the British. During the last six months of the war (it lasted approximately one year) the government executed almost twice as many irregular prisoners as had been killed by

Members of the Irish delegation, including Arthur Griffith (far left) and Michael Collins (seated, center), at the signing of the Irish Free State treaty.

the British from 1916 to 1921. Approximately 665 people were killed and 3,000 were wounded during the period of September 1922 to August 1923.

The war also claimed some high profile victims. On August 22, 1922, Michael Collins was killed when irregulars ambushed his motorcade. And Arthur Griffith, exhausted by the strain of trying to hold his new country together, suffered a fatal heart attack that same month.

However, the deaths of Irish Free State leaders were not enough to allow the irregulars to claim victory. The overwhelming mood of the country was for peace, the public having grown weary of the fighting. In addition, the Roman Catholic Church had thrown its considerable influence behind the government. Thus, on May 24, 1923, De Valera announced that his forces would lay down their arms. He was not, however, willing to concede the basic principles for which he had fought. "Military victory must be allowed to rest for the moment with those who have destroyed the republic,"[23] he announced.

No Refuge from Violence

Despite the fact that it had no direct involvement in the Irish Civil War, Northern Ireland was hardly a refuge from violence. The new country found the initial journey on the road to independence difficult. In the campaign held to elect members to both the British Parliament and its own Parliament, vicious rioting broke out between Unionist (usually Protestant) and nationalist (usually Catholic) factions. Catholics typically suffered the most and were driven from their homes and jobs without mercy. Both sides suffered immensely in Belfast, however. Between July 1920 and June 1922, 452 people were killed in sectarian violence: 267 Catholics and 185 Protestants.

The coffin of Michael Collins is driven through the streets of Dublin. Collins was assassinated by partition opponents.

As if the rioting was not bad enough, an economic war was also occurring. Since the summer of 1920 the IRA, in retaliation for attacks on Catholics during earlier riots, had made certain that goods manufactured in Northern Ireland could not be exported to the Irish Free State. This action served to deepen the divisions between the two Irelands. The Protestants were driven even closer to the English and were alienated from the Catholic minority in Northern Ireland.

For their part, the Catholics were further marginalized. On the one hand, they believed that the establishment of Northern Ireland was meant to keep Protestants in charge there; on the other hand, they hoped that in a few years Ireland would be reunited. As a result, they tended to regard the government as a short-lived phenomenon and chose not to cooperate with it whenever possible.

The outgrowth was that Catholics and Protestants grew more wary and suspicious of each other. Still, an agreement that had been negotiated by Collins in March 1922 to call off the boycott and end IRA activity in return for the rights of the (Catholic) minority being protected in Northern Ireland brought some peace to the region. Furthermore, the outbreak of civil war forced the IRA to concentrate their activities in the remainder of Ireland and not pay as much attention to Northern Ireland as the group might otherwise have done.

New Faces

The end of the Irish Civil War brought some new faces into the realms of power. The deaths of Griffith and Collins resulted in W.T. Cosgrave, another veteran of the Easter 1916 rebellion, becoming head of the Irish government. Kevin O'Higgins, a member of Sinn Féin who had been imprisoned for a time by the British, assumed the post of minister for home affairs.

The rise to prominence of Cosgrave, O'Higgins, and others meant that even though the country was still armed to the teeth and recovering from the trauma of years of war, the framework for the orderly succession of government was being established. This was a crucial first step on the road to democracy for an independent Ireland.

Yet not everyone in Irish public life was so willing to settle into the business of democracy. Eamon De Valera chose to boycott Ireland's government, refusing to participate in the Dáil as long as it recognized any connection to Great Britain.

On December 6, 1922, a constitution for the Irish Free State went into effect. The next day the Parliament of Northern Ireland voted to ask Great Britain to exclude it from the authority of the Irish Free State. This request was swiftly granted. Thus, in the spring of 1923 both Irelands stood, exhausted from years of violence, on the brink of peace.

Making Independence Work

4

With the end of the civil war, Ireland tried to get on with the business of making independence work. But the continued desire for complete freedom from Great Britain, combined with never-ending discontent with the partition that had created Northern Ireland, made peace and prosperity an elusive goal for the Irish to attain.

The Legacy of the Civil War

Even as the Irish Free State struggled with the bitter legacy of the civil war, unrest over the partition of the nation absorbed both Northern Ireland and its island neighbor. While the Catholics in Ulster were expecting to rejoin the rest of Ireland, the Protestants there remained opposed to such a move. Since they were in the majority in Northern Ireland, the weight of Protestant opinions and feelings meant that the country remained tied to Great Britain. Meanwhile, frustrated by the lack of progress in regaining control of the six counties for Ireland, the IRA engaged in various acts of violence to achieve reunification by force.

But the IRA's violence was not successful in joining Ireland with Northern Ireland. If anything, it strengthened the resolve of Northern Ireland's Protestants never to rejoin the rest of Ireland. It also gave the first prime minister of Northern Ireland, James Craig, an opportunity to introduce new classes of police into the country to support the regular police force, the Royal Ulster Constabulary (RUC). These new forces were seen as tools of the Protestant government, leading Catholics to feel that they had no advocates for their viewpoints.

Members of the Royal Ulster Constabulary at Buckingham Palace in London await their official installation by the English king.

In part, the marginalization of Catholics was self-imposed since many deliberately spurned participation in Northern Ireland's institutions, such as the RUC. The RUC's Catholic membership was never more than 16 percent. As a result, whenever sectarian disputes arose, the police tended to side with Protestants, leading to still further alienation of the Catholic minority.

Moving to stifle further nationalist agitation, the Northern Ireland government enacted the Special Powers Act in 1922. This legislation gave the authorities an extraordinarily wide range of powers to curb civil disorder, including the ability to flog suspected nationalist sympathizers. Catholics suspected that these measures were aimed at them, and so the gulf between them and the nation's Protestants continued to widen.

With the failure of both the IRA campaign of violence and the boycotting strategy to achieve reunification, Catholics north and south pinned their hopes for ending partition on the

Boundary Commission. It was widely believed that the Commission's members would recommend moving the two Northern Ireland counties with Catholic majorities back into Ireland. Such a move, many assumed, would leave the north with an economically unworkable four-county area, thereby motivating Protestants to end partition simply in their own self-interest.

Partition Becomes Strengthened

Hopes that the Boundary Commission would effectively end partition were dashed when its report was prematurely leaked in 1925. Many Irish were shocked to learn that the commission was only going to slightly tinker with the border, but otherwise leave it intact. This included keeping the two counties with Catholic majorities—Tyrone and Fermanagh—as part of Northern Ireland.

Like everyone else, members of the Irish Free State's government had been counting on the Boundary Commission to solve the problem of partition. Struggling to establish credible authority in the wake of civil war, the government was worried that Ireland would become inflamed by ongoing strife resulting from partition, and that war would again erupt. So the Irish Free State government hurried into an agreement with Great Britain, accepting the border with Northern Ireland in exchange for writing off Ireland's portion of England's national debt. Meanwhile, Eamon De Valera and his supporters signed a statement recording "unalterable opposition to the partitioning of our country."[24] But since they were boycotting the Irish Parliament in protest over the treaty, their opposition to the agreement had no effect.

The two sides had been defined: De Valera and his faction on one side, firmly against any agreement that kept Ireland tied to England and that strengthened partition; and the remainder of Ireland's politicians on the other side, accepting agreements that were not totally what they sought but tended to inch Ireland further along the road to complete independence from Britain.

Eamon De Valera (seated, third from right) worked to end all remaining ties between Ireland and Britain.

The reason that the head of the Irish Free State, W.T. Cosgrave, accepted the Boundary Commission's report was that he knew that Northern Ireland would never give up any territory without bloodshed—which he was determined to avoid. But his acceptance of reality did not match the mood of his fellow Irish, who expected partition to end.

Making a Break from Great Britain

Yet partition was only one of two major issues preoccupying Irish politics at this time. Besides trying to undo partition, De Valera and his allies were trying to sever all remaining ties with Great Britain and become an independent republic.

One of the first steps Ireland took in that regard was in 1923, when the country took its place in the international body known as the League of Nations. The following year it appointed its own diplomatic representative to the United States. These were both steps that no other dominion-status country had ever taken, and they established the Irish Free State as different from other dominion countries such as Canada and South Africa.

In 1926, at a meeting of representatives from throughout the British Empire, Ireland helped push through a resolution that all nations in the British Empire were equal in status, in no way subordinate to one another in domestic or international affairs. This radically altered the meaning of dominion status, putting the dominion states on a par with England itself. Then, in 1931, the next Imperial Conference produced an even more far-reaching document, the Statute of Westminster, which gave any dominion state the right to unilaterally repeal any United Kingdom legislation binding in its territory. The way was now clear for Ireland to repeal any part of the Anglo-Irish treaty that it disliked.

De Valera's Role

Ireland's change of status from a partially autonomous entity within the British Empire to an independent nation was due in large measure to the resiliency and adaptability of one man, Eamon De Valera. Despite the defeat of his faction in the civil war, De Valera emerged from the fray as one of the most influential politicians in Ireland. He worked tirelessly at making his dream of an Ireland completely free from the yoke of Great Britain a reality. Whether his isolationist policies helped or hurt Ireland in the years following independence is still a matter of debate.

On May 16, 1926, De Valera founded the Fianna Fáil political party. In the general election of June 1927, the new party made a strong showing against Cosgrave's Cumann na nGaedheal party.

Now that they had been elected, De Valera and his followers were left with a decision: Before they could be seated in Ireland's Parliament, all members had to take the oath of allegiance to the British king, as required by the treaty that had created the Irish Free State. This was the same treaty De Valera and his followers had so vehemently opposed, and the oath, in particular, was anathema.

On June 23, 1927, De Valera led his Fianna Fáil followers into the Irish Parliament building. When they refused to take

Eamon De Valera (1882–1975)

Born in New York City, the son of a Spanish music teacher, Vivion De Valera, and an Irish mother, Catherine Coll, Eamon De Valera grew to be the most influential Irish politician of the first half of the twentieth century. When he was two his father died and young Eamon was sent back to Ireland to live with his grandmother, uncle, and aunt because his widowed mother was unable to care for him.

De Valera came to dominate the political scene in Ireland for over forty years. Traveling to early meetings of Fianna Fáil on a white horse and dressed in a flowing black cloak over his long, thin frame, he seemed to many to be a reincarnation of heroic Irish figures of years past. De Valera's following was very much a personal one: People considered themselves followers of De Valera first and followers of Fianna Fáil second.

De Valera was a curious mixture of a revolutionary and a political conservative. He fought against English rule all of his life, including participating in the 1916 Easter Rising. Once he became head of Ireland, however, his policies tended to be conservative and isolationist, maintaining a great deference to the Catholic Church.

In his later years De Valera was almost totally blind, yet he remained in Irish public life until 1973, serving as Ireland's president until then. He died on August 29, 1975.

Eamon De Valera addresses a crowd in America.

the oath, they were locked out of the building. This is the way matters stayed until August, when Cosgrave introduced legislation that sought to make vacant the seats of every Dáil member who did not take the oath.

Unwilling to give up the seat to which he had been elected, De Valera led his followers back into the Dáil on August 10. Then, speaking in Irish, he said, "I am not prepared to take the oath. I am not going to take an oath. I am prepared to put my name down in this book in order to get permission to go into the Dáil, but it has no other significance."[25] Then he pushed aside the Bible on which the oath of allegiance was to be sworn and simply signed his name into the official registry. De Valera later said that he signed his name "in the same way I would sign an autograph in a newspaper."[26] By this simple maneuver, De Valera avoided taking the hated oath and took his seat in the Dáil. Why he could not have done this in 1922, thereby saving the country from a bloody civil war, De Valera never explained.

The Treaty Is Dissolved

Once De Valera was in office, he wasted no time undoing some of the more objectionable provisions of the treaty with Great Britain. A bill was introduced abolishing the oath of allegiance to the British king on April 20, 1932. Then just five years later, in 1937, De Valera pushed through a new constitution that abolished the Irish Free State and renamed the country Ireland, or Éire (Gaelic for "Ireland"). The constitution established Ireland as a country of thirty-two counties, except that it claimed jurisdiction over just twenty-six of those counties, leaving the six Ulster counties out "pending the reintegration of the national territory."[27] Reflecting De Valera's passion for ancient Irish ways and the Gaelic language, the new head of the government was proclaimed to be the an taoiseach (prime minister). The Oireachtas, or Parliament, was established as the legislative body of the country. The Oireachtas had two houses: the Dáil Éireann, or lower chamber, and the Seanad Éireann, or upper chamber.

The new constitution, with its reference to a thirty-two-county nation and the assumption that partition would one day end, infuriated Protestants in Northern Ireland. Also upsetting to the Protestants of Ulster was the reference in the document to the Holy Trinity and to the Catholic Church's role as the guardian of the faith of a great majority of Ireland's citizens.

These two provisions in the constitution made the prospect of uniting both Irelands more remote than ever. To Protestants of the six Ulster counties, the new constitution and its overt references to Catholicism meant that they would be severely handicapped if they ever became part of the rest of Ireland. Protestants came to view southern Ireland with great suspicion, always ready for a takeover attempt.

Economic Hardships

Ireland's efforts to establish itself politically had been made all the more difficult by the fact that the new nation was in a precarious economic situation. By 1932 a worldwide economic depression was seriously affecting Ireland's agriculture-based economy. Between 1928 and 1931 exports of bacon and butter had dropped by half, and egg exports had declined by one-third. Ireland's minuscule manufacturing sector was also affected, with 117 factories closing between 1924 and 1931. This exacerbated the country's chronic unemployment problem.

The Cosgrave government tried to deal with the nation's economic problems by enacting emergency measures, such as reducing the pay of teachers and police in order to cut government spending. To help assure that families would at least have one male adult with a paying job, Cosgrave's government also passed a measure forbidding married women from becoming teachers. These measures were unpopular and contributed to De Valera's and Fianna Fáil's victory in the 1932 elections.

De Valera in Charge

Unfortunately, De Valera's hatred of Great Britain and his isolationist policies worked against Ireland's economic interests. According to a 1926 agreement between the two countries, Britain was supposed to receive an annual sum of money for repayment of loans made to Ireland as part of former British prime minister William Gladstone's Land Act of 1881. When De Valera refused to honor the agreement, Britain tried to obtain this money by slapping high taxes on Irish agricultural imports. Ireland responded by levying similar taxes on British imports, and a trade war between the two began.

Kevin O'Higgins (1892–1927)

At the conclusion of Ireland's civil war, Kevin O'Higgins was the most dominant personality in the Irish government. The minister for home affairs, O'Higgins was a devoted disciple of the Irish Free State's first chief executive, Michael Collins. O'Higgins once admitted that before he acted, he consciously tried to do what Collins would have done.

Flamboyant, profane, ruthless (he ordered the execution of the former best man at his wedding when he was caught working for the anti-treaty side during the civil war), and quick to anger, as minister for home affairs he was responsible for a series of public safety measures that were controversial, such as legislation to restrict the sale of alcoholic beverages.

O'Higgins was also seen as chief beneficiary of a series of public safety acts that gave the new government and its political party, known as Cumann na nGaedheal (Society of Irishmen), a wide range of powers to deal with the IRA, including flogging and imprisonment. On July 10, 1927 O'Higgins was assassinated as he walked to church. His death removed Cumann na nGaedheal's most visible spokesman, and left Eamon De Valera as the Irish politician with the highest public profile.

The struggle took a severe toll on Ireland since Great Britain was a major market for the nation's agricultural products. By 1935 Irish unemployment totaled 138,000, as falling exports meant less demand for Irish goods and thus less work for everyone. In 1931, before the start of the trade war, unemployment had been 28,934. Finally, in 1938 De Valera and British prime minister Neville Chamberlain negotiated an end to the conflict.

Ireland had been particularly vulnerable to a trade war because of its great dependence on agricultural exports. Most of the island's factories were located in Northern Ireland, with the result that Ireland was once described by a writer as "a country which looked as if it had been bypassed altogether by the Industrial Revolution."[28] Much of the manufacturing that was located in Ireland was still related to agriculture, such as brewing, distilling, bacon curing, and butter making. Any dispute that affected demand for its agricultural products was guaranteed to deal a hammer blow to the nation's economy.

Hampering Ireland's ability to become more manufacturing-oriented was the fact that workers were in short supply because of the continual emigration of Irish men and women from their own country. This emigration had begun during the Potato Famine years and had held steady in the decades that followed. The population of Ireland had shrunk from a high of approximately 6.5 million in 1841 to an estimated 3.2 million in 1901. By 1926 it had sunk to about 2.9 million. In some villages entire generations were gone. So, faced with potential problems hiring the needed workers, manufacturers shunned Ireland as a place to invest in new plants. Thus, Ireland was faced with a paradox. The nation had an economy that needed to be diversified by introducing more manufacturing, but it did not have enough workers to support new industries.

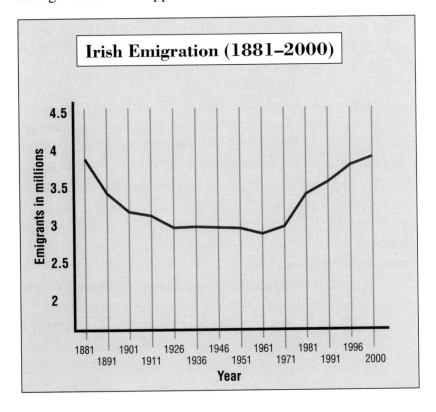

Meanwhile, Northern Ireland, thanks to its status as a part of the United Kingdom, had been relatively unaffected by the trade dispute. Yet Northern Ireland still endured relentless poverty and a standard of living well below that of Great Britain. In 1938, for example, 87 percent of houses in rural areas did not have running water.

Ominously, poverty in Northern Ireland affected the nation's Catholics disproportionately. The government continued to emphasize the dominant position of the Protestant religion in the country, which had the effect of further alienating the Catholic minority. The leader of Northern Ireland, James Craig, said in 1934, "All I boast is that we are a Protestant parliament and a Protestant state."[29] Due to comments like this, Catholics were well aware of which religious class enjoyed favored status in Northern Ireland.

World War II

Any hopes Ireland had of addressing some of its long-standing difficulties were dealt another setback by World War II.

In particular, Ireland's prickly relations with Great Britain and the divisions between Ireland and Northern Ireland were brought into sharper focus by World War II. Ireland declared its neutrality one day after Germany invaded Poland on September 1, 1939. It was a neutrality, however, tilted toward the Allies. For example, Allied fighter pilots who landed in Ireland had their planes refueled and were allowed to proceed. By contrast, German airmen who landed in Ireland were imprisoned. Just as in World War I, the Irish supported the Allies with their blood. It is estimated that fifty thousand Irishmen were serving in the British armed forces at the end of the war.

Still, Ireland's neutrality exacerbated ill feelings with Great Britain. England could not understand why Ireland refused to join in fighting the Nazis. In the final days of the war, De Valera offended many in Great Britain by signing a book of condolence at the German embassy when Adolf Hitler died.

Irish soldiers, serving for the British Army, study wartime strategy.

Ireland's neutrality also widened the gulf between it and Northern Ireland, which remained loyal and supported Great Britain during the war. As a steadfast ally of Great Britain, Northern Ireland's aircraft and shipping industries benefited both nations. Due in part to production of war materiel, an economic revival began in Northern Ireland. Between 1938 and 1947, for example, per capita income rose by 84 percent there. This figure was six times higher than that for Ireland.

The Birth of the Irish Republic

In the years following World War II, Ireland's politicians set about further defining Irish independence. Although it had long been De Valera's dream to establish an independent Irish republic, it was John Costello, the leader of a coalition of political parties opposed to Fianna Fáil, who actually accomplished that feat when he was Ireland's taoiseach. Since 1937 Ireland had been officially a member of the British Commonwealth, an organization of nations that had once been part of the British Empire. Ironically, it was De Valera's political party, Fianna Fáil, that opposed leaving the commonwealth and establishing a republic. The official position of Fianna Fáil was that by leading Ireland out of the commonwealth, Costello was making it much more difficult to end partition.

Regardless of such arguments, on April 18, 1949, the anniversary of the 1916 Easter Rising, Ireland officially left the British Commonwealth and became a completely independent nation. In retaliation for Ireland's move, Britain passed a law stating that Northern Ireland would never cease being part of the United Kingdom without the consent of the Northern Ireland Parliament. Thus, a partition that had once been considered temporary became even more permanent.

Economies During the 1950s and 1960s

Along with political independence, Ireland also began to achieve economic independence during the post–World War II era by diversifying its economy. Ireland ended its reliance primarily on an agricultural economy through a campaign of domestic investment in industry and a major effort to attract foreign investment. The campaign was spearheaded by Sean

John Aloysius Costello (1891–1976)

John Aloysius Costello was the Irish prime minister who finally took Ireland out of the British Commonwealth in 1949. Born in Dublin, he was a lawyer and an Irish patriot. He participated in the Easter Rising of 1916. From 1926 until 1932 he was the attorney general of the Irish Free State, and he also served as the country's delegate to the League of Nations. In 1948 he was elected prime minister, replacing Eamon De Valera. Defeated by De Valera for prime minister in 1951, Costello was reelected prime minister in 1954, serving until 1957. He then served as leader of the opposition party until 1959.

Lemass, taoiseach from 1959 to 1966 and another veteran of the Easter Rising who, at age sixteen, had been the youngest rebel in the conflict. The other initiator of the campaign was Kenneth Whitaker, secretary of the Finance Department, who developed a blueprint for manufacturing expansion. The planning by Lemass and Whitaker paid off. Between 1959 and 1968 industrial output rose by 82 percent. By 1964 more than two hundred factories had been started, many of them with foreign participation.

The improving economic opportunities led to a decline in emigration in Ireland for the first time since the Potato Famine days. The 1966 census showed an increase in the population of over sixty thousand, and a decrease in yearly emigration from nearly sixty thousand to about twelve thousand between 1962 and 1963.

This economic resurgence could not have come too quickly for many of the inhabitants of Ireland. Many were living in primitive conditions. Of the 676,402 dwellings in Ireland in 1961, just one-third had hot water, and less than half had indoor toilets.

Northern Ireland's economy enjoyed boom times during the 1950s and 1960s as well. Great Britain began offering its citizens such things as government-financed health care and schooling, and it also offered those services to Northern Ireland, creating still more jobs in the process. Another reason for Northern Ireland's gathering economic momentum was that Great Britain also offered government grants to both modernize and encourage industry.

A Continuing Preoccupation with Partition

Yet hanging over both Ireland and Northern Ireland was lingering resentment regarding partition. In 1956 the IRA began a new campaign of violence in Northern Ireland with the stated objective of ending partition.

The IRA's campaign ended without achieving its objective; the renewed violence claimed one political victim, however.

When Taoiseach Costello asked the Dáil for the authority to deal decisively with the IRA, political opponents not only denied him that but also went on to bring down his government.

In Northern Ireland, meanwhile, extremists were equally active. During his tenure as Northern Ireland's prime minister from 1963 to 1969, Terence O'Neill began to cautiously reach out to Catholic constituents by visiting Catholic schools. He also met with Ireland's leader, Sean Lemass, to try and improve relations between the two countries.

These conciliatory gestures were, however, met with angry reactions from some Protestants. In particular, a Presbyterian minister named Ian Paisley heckled O'Neill at public meetings, accusing him of "moving toward Rome"[30]—that is, of becoming too close to Catholics, whose spiritual leader, the pope, resides in Rome.

Religious or Political?

The reaction of Paisley to even modest gestures of conciliation was a prime example of the problems any attempt to end partition might entail. Just below the surface of every political dispute lay religion.

In fact, religion underlies everyday life in Ireland to such a degree that a tale is told of a census taker who, when he asked an Irishman to identify his religious affiliation, was told that the respondent was an agnostic. Quizzically, the census taker asked if the man was a Catholic agnostic or a Protestant one. This lighthearted anecdote masks the serious role that religion plays in Irish politics. During the late 1960s, religious violence would once again dominate the Irish political scene.

Renewed Conflict 5

Even as the Republic of Ireland gradually achieved a modest level of prosperity, Northern Ireland found itself in the midst of a devastating civil conflict. Fed up with being treated as second-class citizens, the Catholic minority in that country began pushing for equal rights with the ruling Protestants. Extremist Protestants and Catholics both formed militias and set out to resolve through violence what they saw as long-standing grievances. A seemingly endless cycle of score settling began, causing enormous suffering throughout Ulster.

A Civil Rights March

On October 5 and 6, 1968, in the Northern Ireland city of Londonderry, a group of Catholics set off on a protest march. The marchers were attempting to call attention to housing and employment discrimination against Catholics as well as the rigging of the local election process, which tended to keep the Protestant Unionist Party in power even in districts where the Protestants were in the minority. When the Catholics refused to abide by the Northern Ireland custom that dictated that Catholics do not march through Protestant parts of a town and vice versa, police broke up the demonstration using what many observers considered excessive force. With pressure mounting for a redress of these wrongs to the Catholics, Northern Ireland's prime minister, Terence O'Neill, broadcast an address in which he said that Ulster was on the brink of chaos.

O'Neill Resigns

For years O'Neill had been aware of the inequities suffered by Catholics, and he had been working to redress some of their grievances in areas such as housing, elections, and employment. But O'Neill found that he had overestimated the support for his reforms. When he called for elections early in 1969 to gain support for his reform efforts, he came within 1,414 votes of losing his seat in Parliament to Ian Paisley, the extremist leader of the Protestants who opposed any concessions to the country's Catholics.

Interpreting the close call as a signal that the voters lacked confidence in his leadership, O'Neill resigned as prime minister late in April. He was replaced by James Dawson Chichester-Clark, who nevertheless continued with O'Neill's reforms.

A Parade Leads to New Violence

Chichester-Clark's election cooled tensions, but in August 1969 they heated up once again. As before, the provocation was a parade, this time by Protestants who chose to march through predominantly Catholic neighborhoods of Londonderry. Once again, rioting broke out between the two factions. The rioting

Members of the Royal Ulster Constabulary and civil rights demonstrators clashed in Londonderry in October 1968.

soon spread to Belfast, where over seven hundred people were injured.

It was soon apparent that civil authority had broken down. In cities such as Belfast and Londonderry, certain neighborhoods were barricaded off by extremist Catholic and Protestant groups; behind those barricades no police authority was recognized, and gun-toting militiamen represented the only law enforcement available.

Soon Britain was once again drawn into the problems of Northern Ireland. The local police proved powerless to stop the escalating violence, so the British government sent troops to Northern Ireland to keep the peace. At the same time, the British also tried to address some of the Catholics' complaints by implementing political and housing reforms. But the violence continued as Protestants complained that too much was being given away and Catholics complained that the reforms failed to go far enough.

The Provisional IRA

The so-called Provisional IRA, or the Provos, played a major role in the renewal of Northern Ireland violence. The Provos were a wing of the IRA that had broken away from the main group sometime during the 1960s.

Initially the Provos' violence met with little sympathy from the Catholic citizens of Northern Ireland. Even though they were being discriminated against by the ruling Protestants, these people welcomed the arrival of British troops. They hoped that the troops would be fairer toward them than the Northern Ireland police had been, particularly the special police unit called the B Specials. But the troops proved to be as biased against the Catholics as the police, and soon the sympathies of Northern Ireland's Catholics shifted to the Provos.

But the violent tactics used by the Provos backfired. Instead of causing the Catholics to be treated more fairly, they just provoked Protestant groups loyal to England to initiate their own attacks in retaliation. Thus, Northern Ireland was trapped in a deadly cycle of violence and reprisals.

Another Bloody Sunday

Eventually, the violence claimed another victim: civil liberties. Faced with increasing pressure to do something about the Provos, the Northern Ireland government introduced a policy of internment without trial in August 1971. Exercising their new powers, British soldiers and Northern Ireland's police rounded up 342 people, mainly Catholics who favored reunification with the Republic of Ireland. Allegations of mistreatment of internees at the hands of the British army quickly spread. Both the internment policy and the rumors of abuse further inflamed the Catholic community.

Relations between Catholics, Protestants, and the British army reached an all-time low on Sunday, January 30, 1972. That day, which became known as yet another "Bloody Sunday," British paratroopers shot and killed thirteen unarmed Catholic protesters during a march in Londonderry. A fourteenth person later died of injuries. Some observers questioned

Riot police in Londonderry flee as gasoline bombs explode.

the circumstances, but the official inquiry by the British government into the incident exonerated the paratroopers involved, saying that since the protesters had handled guns earlier in the day, the shootings were justified.

Violence Spreads to England

Civil unrest continued to worsen. As order continued to deteriorate, the British government suspended the Northern Ireland Parliament in March 1972 and imposed direct rule on the nation. A new office in the British government—secretary of state for Northern Ireland—was established to directly deal with the problems in that country. It was hoped that by ruling the country directly from England, the British government could stop the violence and reestablish law and order.

As part of their effort to rein in terrorism, the British tried holding peace talks with the various IRA factions, but these negotiations failed to stem the violence. The outcome, in fact, was still more violence. On July 21, 1972, the Provos detonated a staggering twenty-two bombs in Belfast, killing nine civilians. Despite Britain's best efforts, they had not succeeded in stopping the terrorist attacks. And, once they directly involved themselves in Northern Ireland, the British also became targets of Provo violence at home. In 1973 the Provos began setting off bombs in Great Britain on the assumption that a terror campaign there would force the British government to abandon its support of Northern Ireland and allow Ulster to be reunited with the Republic of Ireland.

The Sunningdale Experiment

Rather than abandon Northern Ireland, the British tried yet again to find a political settlement. In December 1973 leaders from Britian, Northern Ireland, and the Irish republic responded to the Provos' bombing campaign by meeting at a mansion outside of London known as Sunningdale and drafted what became known as the Sunningdale agreement. The accord established the Council of Ireland, which would contain members from both Irelands who would exercise a consultative role

British troops in Northern Ireland take cover behind armored cars during a demonstration in January 1972.

in Northern Ireland's affairs. The agreement also stated that Northern Ireland would remain a part of the United Kingdom until a majority of voters in the country decided otherwise.

The Council of Ireland offered an opportunity for power sharing and reconciliation in Northern Ireland, but the agreement never got the chance to take effect. Northern Ireland Protestants, alarmed that the council represented the first steps toward Catholics gaining more control of their country, pressured Northern Ireland's prime minister, Brian Faulkner, to oppose the Sunningdale accord.

In May 1974, despite Faulkner's opposition, the Northern Ireland Assembly came together again and conditionally approved the Sunningdale agreement. In protest, a group calling itself the Ulster Worker's Council called for a strike that virtually paralyzed Belfast. British troops were forced to operate electrical generating plants, gas stations, and other vital facilities. Faced with widespread public support for the strikers, the British government abandoned the Sunningdale agreement, which then collapsed.

Bombings and terrorism by the Provos continued for the next several years, both in and out of Northern Ireland. Their targets varied, and sometimes the bombings took innocent lives. The highest profile victim of the violence was Lord Louis Mountbatten, formerly the supreme Allied commander for Southeast Asia during World War II and the uncle of Britain's Queen Elizabeth II. He was killed on August 27,

Hunger Strikes

The British chose to treat the bombings committed by the Provisional IRA as crimes, and the bombers—when they could catch them—as common criminals. The IRA prisoners wanted to be classified as political prisoners, but the British government of Prime Minister Margaret Thatcher refused. In October 1980 the prisoners went on a hunger strike to emphasize their demands. That December the strikes temporarily halted, but they were resumed again in March 1981 by an IRA prisoner named Bobby Sands and fifteen others. The Provos publicized Sands's actions, and he received a great deal of public support both in Northern Ireland and in other countries. Ultimately, Sands starved himself to death, as did nine other Provos.

Masked members of the IRA accompany the coffin of Bobby Sands, who died after a hunger strike in jail.

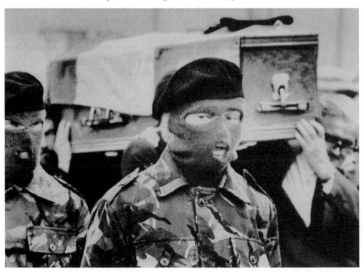

The funeral of Lord Mountbatten, who was killed when an IRA bomb exploded aboard his fishing yacht.

1979—along with three other people, including his fourteen-year-old grandson—on his fishing boat, which he was using for recreation off the coast of the city of Mullaghmore in the Irish republic.

Throughout the 1980s, Northern Ireland continued to stumble through a nightmarish existence. Protestant and Catholic extremists were at each other's throats, the British government seemed powerless to protect them, and the citizenry knew that a Provisional IRA bomb could explode any minute, at any place, and there was nothing they could do about it.

International Relations and the Irish Republic

Meanwhile, the Irish republic continued to walk a tightrope throughout the 1970s and 1980s: The government tried to bring peace to Northern Ireland by denouncing terrorism, but by the same token, it did not oppose terrorism so strongly as to anger the many IRA supporters and Irish nationalists among its own people. Ireland's position was made particularly difficult by the fact that terrorists from Northern Ireland would often take refuge in the Irish republic and stash weapons and explosives there.

In 1972 the Dáil showed that it was serious about taking the gun out of Irish politics by requiring the surrender of all weapons in the Irish republic. This was an unprecedented step for a nation in which gun ownership was widespread. But the outcome of the order was unclear at best, as many Irish continued to keep guns in defiance of the order.

The Irish republic had other concerns as well, largely centered on strengthening its economy. One means of accomplishing this objective was to gain membership in the European Economic Community—what today is known as the European Union (EU). The EU is an organization of European nations that works to promote and expand cooperation among its members in areas such as economics, trade, foreign policy, and security. The primary benefit for Ireland was that membership would provide access to markets besides Great Britain, allowing it to diversify its economy still more.

After Ireland was admitted on January 1, 1991, membership in the EU proved to be a boon for Irish farmers. Taking out newly available loans with their land as collateral, farmers suddenly were able to buy all of the latest modern conveniences for their homes, such as color televisions and other appliances. For their farms, they were able to buy modern milking machines, new barns, and a host of other improvements that boosted their productivity.

The Ongoing Church Influence

Ireland's membership in the EU and its subsequent prosperity were evidence that it had clearly made political independence work, but by the 1980s many Irish began to feel that they also needed to free their society from what often seemed the undue influence of the Catholic Church in the nation's affairs.

European Union foreign ministers. Membership in the European Union proved a boon to Irish farmers.

Ireland had already taken a first step toward reducing the church's presence in everyday life when, in 1967, the government relaxed its censorship policies, which had existed since 1929 with the tacit support of the church. So stringent had censorship been that even books by such great writers as Ernest Hemingway, William Faulkner, Thomas Mann, George Orwell, F. Scott Fitzgerald, and Somerset Maugham had been banned. Magazines and newspapers had also been operating under the censorship requirements.

Far more divisive than censorship was the issue of whether to legalize divorce. Since 1937 divorce had been specifically prohibited in the constitution that Eamon De Valera had drafted. In 1986 the taoiseach, Garret FitzGerald, called for a referendum on making divorce legal. The proposal failed: sixty-three percent of those who went to the polls voted against lifting the ban. Part of the reason that the proposed amendment did not pass was opposition from the Catholic Church, whose leaders, despite an agreement with FitzGerald not to campaign against the proposal, were still able to rally public opinion.

Church influence on the Irish government was most tested in relation to policies regarding sexual conduct. Laws prohibited the sale and importation of contraceptives; even advocating the use of contraceptives had been illegal since 1929. In February 1985 the government introduced a bill that lifted the restrictions on the sale of contraceptives to a person over eighteen years of age. Despite dire predictions from clergymen and others that such a law would lead to sexual promiscuity, the Dáil narrowly passed the law.

Church teachings continued to influence some government policies, however. Abortion, for example, had long been banned in Ireland. However, Catholic organizations grew concerned that the trend toward easing such restrictions in Europe and the United States might someday spread to Ireland, and they proposed strengthening the ban by adding it to the constitution.

The campaign divided the Irish, but the proposed amendment passed. The amendment read, "Nothing in the Constitution shall be invoked to invalidate or to deprive of force or effect a provision of the law on the grounds that it prohibits abortion."[31] In other words, restrictions on abortions could not be struck down by courts on constitutional grounds.

The Anglo-Irish Agreement

As much as social issues concerned Ireland, the ongoing conflict in Northern Ireland continued to be of paramount importance in Irish politics.

Margaret Thatcher (1925–   )

Margaret Thatcher was the first woman to become prime minister of Great Britain (1979–1990). A member of the Conservative Party, she was first elected to the House of Commons in 1959. Thatcher served as the minister of education and science during Prime Minister Edward Heath's government. She challenged Heath for the Conservative Party leadership and won the post in 1975. In 1979 she was elected prime minister. Throughout her tenure as prime minister, Thatcher was a hard-line foe of Irish extremists looking to reunite Ireland and Northern Ireland through violence. She resigned her post in 1990.

In mid-November 1985 the British prime minister, Margaret Thatcher, and taoiseach FitzGerald signed the Anglo-Irish Agreement. The agreement set forth several important points. First, it stated that no change could occur in Northern Ireland's political status without the consent of the people living there. Therefore, bombings and other terrorist tactics by the Provos were not going to force the country to rejoin the rest of Ireland.

Secondly, the pact established a conference whereby British and Irish representatives could meet and discuss concerns about matters relating to Northern Ireland. Ireland was also granted the right to recommend—but not appoint—people to serve in agencies that dealt with Northern Ireland, such as the Fair Employment Agency and the Northern Ireland Police Authority.

The agreement gave the Irish government the ability to represent the concerns of the nationalists inside both Northern Ireland and Ireland. Although the Unionists in Northern Ireland rejected the pact, feeling that it gave Ireland a voice in their country's affairs and reduced British control, the agreement remained in effect. Still, as the final decade of the twentieth century dawned, it remained to be seen how far both Irelands had progressed on the path to peace.

Ireland at a Crossroad

As the last decade of the twentieth century began, both Irelands were at a turning point. One path appeared to offer lasting peace while the other seemed to lead to renewed violence, a violence that had framed so much of each country's history.

The 1990s Start Off Badly

The 1990s did not start off on a hopeful note. Because of continued unrest, British soldiers were still patrolling the streets of the Northern Ireland cities of Londonderry and Belfast. The Provos were still active, exploding bombs throughout Ulster as well as in England. To prove that no one was safe, in February 1991 the IRA fired a mortar shell that landed in the back garden of 10 Downing Street in London, the home of the British prime minister. Then, in April 1992, a bomb exploded in London's financial district, killing three people.

But the bombing that produced the most outrage occurred on November 2, 1991, when an IRA explosion rocked the military wing of a hospital in southern Belfast. Unfortunately, the bomb injured several children in a nearby civilian hospital ward. As television viewers watched rescue workers dig out children from the hospital's rubble, cries for interning suspected terrorists grew louder, both in England and in Northern Ireland.

For all of the revulsion that the hospital bombing caused, it seemed like the return to the mayhem of the early 1970s in Northern Ireland. Unionist and IRA death squads roamed the streets of Northern Ireland's major cities, seemingly killing at random. In one particularly horrific incident, a Catholic mother and her sixteen-year-old daughter were burned to death when

Fire engines respond to a bomb explosion at Britain's Parliament building. The IRA used terror bombings in the 1970s to force reunification of Ireland.

Unionists attacked their home. Then, in January 1992, a bomb planted by the Provos blew up a bus carrying Protestant construction workers, killing eight.

But in the midst of all of this bloodshed, there was some progress toward peace. First, in August 1992, the British government banned the Ulster Defense Association, the Unionist equivalent of the IRA. This was a move many in Northern Ireland, particularly the nationalists, had been calling for as a precondition to peace. After all, it was reasoned, how could there be peace with one side's terrorist group free to operate under the protection of the law?

Brooke Sounds a Hopeful Note

The first moves toward peace had actually begun several years earlier. In 1989 Peter Brooke, who was Great Britain's secretary of state for Northern Ireland, declared that the IRA was too well organized to be beaten and said that the British government would be "flexible and imaginative"[32] in its response to a cessation of violence by the terrorist group.

Then, in early November 1990, Brooke gave a speech in which he noted that partition was "an acknowledgement of reality, not an assertion of national self-interest."[33] In essence, Brooke was saying that Britain would not stand in the way of Irish unity if it came about with the consent of the people of Northern Ireland.

Brooke's gentler tone was reinforced later that month when John Major replaced Margaret Thatcher as Britain's prime minister. Thatcher had long been an enemy of the IRA for her hardline attitude toward them, and the IRA hoped that her successor would be more conciliatory.

Those hopes, however, seemed unfulfilled. Although Major allowed Brooke to begin holding talks with some of the groups involved in the Northern Ireland dispute, such as the Ulster Unionist Party, the IRA's political wing, Sinn Féin, was excluded, and the talks faltered as a result.

Then, in December 1992, Brooke's successor, Sir Patrick Mayhew, announced that if the IRA declared a cease-fire, Sinn Féin could be included in the talks. It took almost two years of delicate negotiations, but on August 31, 1994, the IRA issued a statement that read:

> In order to enhance the democratic peace process and underline our definitive commitment to its success the leadership of Oglaigh na hEireann [Irish Republican Army] have decided that as of midnight 31 August, there will be a complete cessation of military operations. All our units have been instructed accordingly.[34]

In October 1994 the Unionist paramilitary organizations followed the IRA's lead in declaring a cease-fire. Peace finally came to the embattled country of Northern Ireland.

For many in Northern Ireland, Christmas 1994 truly represented a time of hope and goodwill that had not been seen or felt in that country for many years. The smothering crush of security that had been in force for years was relaxed: Soldiers still patrolled city streets, but they did so without helmets; and police officers discarded their bulletproof vests. Holiday shoppers thronged department stores—for the first time in years without fear of terrorists' bombs exploding outside. Whereas cars had previously been banned from parking downtown for fear of an automobile being booby-trapped with a bomb, now parking was allowed much closer to the centers of town. People stayed out late and did not feel the need to rush home before dark.

The Peace Process Stumbles

The peace process quickly hit some snags, however. On March 7, 1995, Mayhew listed three conditions that the IRA had to abide by before Sinn Féin would be allowed to participate in the peace talks. The conditions were that the IRA must agree in principle to

A schoolgirl in Belfast walks past a wall bearing the slogan, "Not a Bullet," referring to the IRA's refusal to give up their weapons before beginning peace talks.

disarm; there must be agreement on how to go about disarming; and there must be what he called a confidence-building gesture: a token gesture of disarmament that could be taken as evidence that the IRA was serious. Furious over these added conditions, the IRA rejected the notion that it should give up its weapons, and the idea of disarming, or decommissioning of weapons as it was known, threatened to wreck the fragile peace process.

America Becomes Involved

Meanwhile, the United States had entered the tangled web of Northern Ireland in a bid to broker a peace agreement. At the urging of Massachusetts senator Edward Kennedy and his sister Jean Kennedy Smith, who was serving as the U.S. ambassador to Ireland, President Bill Clinton made the search for peace in Northern Ireland one of his administration's top priorities. To this end, in 1994 Clinton rejected the advice of both America's State Department and England's government and gave a visa to Gerry Adams, president of Sinn Féin, to visit America. This sent the signal to all parties that the American government considered Adams a legitimate political leader, not a terrorist outlaw, and worthy of being included in negotiations over Northern Ireland's future.

Then, in December 1994, Clinton again demonstrated his belief in Adams's legitimacy by threatening to keep U.S. diplomat Ron Brown from attending a Belfast investment conference if the British barred Adams from attending, as they were threatening to do. England relented, and both men attended the conference.

Clinton next demonstrated his acceptance of Adams by including the Sinn Féin leader as one of his guests at a St. Patrick's Day celebration in 1995, to which representatives of other Irish political parties, such as the Unionists, were also invited.

Then, in late November 1995, Clinton further signaled his interest in Northern Ireland by visiting that country. Clinton's visit was a popular success, and the crowds that turned out to

President Bill Clinton (right) shakes hands with Sinn Féin president Gerry Adams.

greet the American president showed that Northern Ireland's citizens supported his peace efforts.

Mitchell's Contribution

But America's involvement in the search for peace in Northern Ireland was more substantial than simply enhancing Sinn Féin's prestige or Clinton's whirlwind tour of the country. In 1994 Clinton had also appointed George Mitchell, a former U.S. senator from Maine, as a special economic envoy to Ireland. Mitchell had established a reputation as a patient man willing to listen, and he used those attributes in his new role. Then, in 1995, Clinton appointed Mitchell chairman of a commission whose mandate was to find a diplomatic means to end violence in Northern Ireland.

It was a difficult job for anyone to undertake, and Mitchell had his hands full. He had to listen to the viewpoints of Northern Ireland's approximately one dozen political parties, as well as respect the wishes of Great Britain.

In late January 1996 Mitchell's commission published its report. It stated that decommissioning of the IRA's weapons should not be a precondition to beginning peace talks, and that elections should be held in Northern Ireland to establish which political parties had enough popular support to justify their inclusion in the peace talks.

But despite the report's obvious attempts to achieve a compromise among the various parties, it received a chilly reception. Britain's prime minister, John Major, rejected the report, and Sinn Féin dismissed elections as merely a tactic to delay peace talks.

The stage was now set for a resumption of violence, and on February 9, 1996, an IRA-planted car bomb exploded in a London parking garage. The blast killed two people and injured one hundred others.

If the IRA thought bombing would further its cause, the organization miscalculated. Over 150,000 of Northern Ireland's people, Catholics and Protestants alike, telephoned Belfast's two morning newspapers in the weeks that followed demanding an end to the violence and a restoration of the cease-fire.

Still, the IRA persisted in its campaign, and the violence continued until July 20, 1997. By that time, Britain's government was under the leadership of the Labour Party's Tony Blair, who indicated his desire to restart the peace talks—this time with Sinn Féin present. On September 15, 1997, Adams and other Sinn Féin leaders joined the talks. For the first time since Michael Collins had negotiated with the British government in 1921, IRA representatives had direct contact with British leaders.

A Historic Agreement

The peace talks, under the guidance of George Mitchell, dragged on until April 1998, threatening many times to derail.

George Mitchell (1933–   )

George Mitchell played a significant role in the Good Friday peace accord.

Born in Waterville, Maine, Mitchell became a high-profile member of the Democratic Party and completed Senator Edmund Muskie's term when Muskie was named secretary of state by President Jimmy Carter in 1980. Mitchell subsequently was elected to the Senate in his own right, and served there until 1995.

That year, President Bill Clinton named him an economic adviser for Northern Ireland. Mitchell then was appointed chairperson of negotiations to end the violence in Northern Ireland. In April 1998 these negotiations produced the Good Friday peace agreement. Mitchell was credited for his patience, willingness to listen, and his ability to keep all parties focused during the negotiations.

Mitchell eventually set a deadline of April 9 to complete the talks, and everybody strove furiously to meet it. At one point Blair even physically blocked the door to prevent David Trimble, the Unionist Party leader, from walking out of the talks. At the eleventh hour, President Clinton intervened, calling the various leaders involved on the telephone in order to keep the talks moving forward. Ireland's taoiseach, Bertie Ahern, also participated in the negotiations, as everyone seemed to realize that they represented a rare opportunity to bring peace to Northern Ireland.

Finally, on Good Friday, April 10, 1998, an agreement was reached. It stated that a new 108-seat assembly would be elected in Northern Ireland, with Catholics guaranteed representation, ending over two decades of direct British rule. The agreement also stated that a bill of rights would be drawn up protecting the civil liberties of the Catholic minority, and that the North-South Council would be formed with members from both Irelands to deal with issues of common concern, such as transportation and agriculture.

The Irish republic contributed to the peace process by eliminating two articles from its 1937 constitution: The first asserted Ireland's right to govern the entire island, and the second stated that it was Ireland's duty to seek reunification with Northern Ireland. All parties reaffirmed that it was the right of a majority of Northern Ireland's citizens to decide the nation's political future.

The agreement was approved by 94 percent of the voters of Ireland, and 71 percent of Northern Ireland's voters. On June 25, 1998, elections were held for the new Northern Ireland Assembly. The Unionist Party, led by Trimble, won twenty-eight seats—the best showing. The Social Democratic and Labour Party, headed by John Hume, won twenty-four seats; and Ian Paisley's Democratic Unionist Party, which had opposed the agreement but had reluctantly participated in the election, won twenty seats. Sinn Féin won eighteen seats. Trimble, because his party won the most seats, was named the prime minister of the government.

The Peace Agreement in Peril

As much as people yearned for peace to finally come to all of Ireland, both north and south, in the spring of 2001 another crisis threatened the fragile Good Friday peace agreement. Elections were being held to determine Northern Ireland's representation in the British Parliament. Trimble, hoping to galvanize support for his Ulster Unionist Party, had vowed during the election campaign to resign his leadership of the

David Trimble, the leader of the Ulster Unionist Party.

Northern Ireland government if the IRA did not start to disarm by July 1, 2001. When July 1 came and the IRA did not disarm, Trimble followed through on his threat. As a result, the entire Good Friday peace agreement was at risk of falling apart. The specter of renewed violence between Catholics and Protestants loomed over the country.

Eventually, in the fall of 2001, the IRA began decommissioning its weapons, and the peace process once again seemed on track. The road to a lasting settlement, however, promised to be a perilous one, and further setbacks were seen as likely.

Breaking Out of the Cocoon

Even as it participated in the process of building peace for its island neighbor, the Irish republic faced transitions of its own.

Ireland spent much of the 1990s continuing to break out of its isolationist cocoon and attract new industry and investment. Although farming was still an important occupation in the country, its prominence was diminishing. Among the industries that the country could now support were meatpacking, brewing and distilling, grain milling, sugar refining, the manufacture of office machinery and data-processing equipment, and chemicals. In fact, Ireland's effort to diversify was so successful that by the year 2000, manufacturing had eclipsed agriculture in importance in the Irish economy.

In addition to working to modernize and diversify its economy, Ireland continued its attempt to recast itself as a modern, secular society. Inevitably, this led to some conflict over the influence of the Roman Catholic Church on public policy. For example, alarmed by the spread of AIDS, the government legalized the sale of condoms and other contraceptives in 1993. In February 1997 a law legalizing divorce under certain circumstances went into effect in Ireland. Both of these measures passed despite the disapproval of church leaders.

Still a Country of Contrasts

As Ireland entered the twenty-first century, it was still a country of contrasts. Green and sparsely inhabited in some areas, Ireland remained a place where it was possible to find villages made up of thatch-roofed cottages that seemed unchanged since the nineteenth century. Yet within that pastoral scene was the sight of new factories springing up that produced a host of modern products such as those for the telecommunications industry.

Overshadowing everything were the questions of relations with Northern Ireland and what direction they would take—peaceful or acrimonious. The future of Ireland remains, therefore, shrouded in uncertainty. Samuel Johnson, the eighteenth-century British author and critic, once noted, "The Irish are a fair people. They never speak well of one another."[35] Whether this observation is simply a grim joke or a portent of the future for Ireland is yet to be decided.

Notes

Chapter One: A Nation Defined by Struggle

1. Quoted in Michael L. Landon, *Erin and Britannia*. Chicago: Nelson-Hall, 1981, p. 22.

2. Quoted in Dervla Murphy, *Ireland*. Salem, NH: Salem House, 1985, p. 8.

3. Quoted in Murphy, *Ireland,* p. 84.

4. Quoted in Landon, *Erin and Britannia,* p. 81.

5. Quoted in Tony Gray, *The Irish Answer*. Boston: Little, Brown, 1966, p. 31.

6. Quoted in Oliver MacDonagh, *Ireland*. Englewood Cliffs, NJ: Prentice-Hall, 1968, p. 4.

7. Quoted in K.S. Daly, *Ireland*. Berkeley, CA: Ten Speed, 1994, p. 148.

8. Quoted in Magnus Magnusson, *Landlord or Tenant?* London: Bodley Head, 1978, p. 50.

9. Quoted in Magnusson, *Landlord or Tenant?* p. 71.

10. Quoted in MacDonagh, *Ireland,* p. 45.

Chapter Two: Battles for Independence

11. Quoted in Donald S. Connery, *The Irish*. New York: Simon and Schuster, 1968, p. 58.

12. Quoted in J.C. Beckett, *The Making of Modern Ireland*. New York: Alfred A. Knopf, 1966, p. 377.

13. Quoted in Magnusson, *Landlord or Tenant?* p. 104.

14. Quoted in Magnusson, *Landlord or Tenant?* p. 124.

15. Quoted in Beckett, *The Making of Modern Ireland,* p. 427.

16. Quoted in Magnusson, *Landlord or Tenant?* p. 128.

17. Quoted in Murphy, *Ireland,* p. 104.

18. Quoted in Beckett, *The Making of Modern Ireland,* p. 441.

Chapter Three: Birth of Two Nations
19. Quoted in Gray, *The Irish Answer,* p. 45.

20. Quoted in Peter Neville, *A Traveler's History of Ireland.* New York: Interlink Books, 1997, p. 183.

21. Quoted in Timothy Patrick Coogan, *Ireland Since the Rising.* New York: Frederick A. Praeger, 1966, p. 35.

22. Quoted in Beckett, *The Making of Modern Ireland,* p. 452.

23. Quoted in Beckett, *The Making of Modern Ireland,* p. 459.

Chapter Four: Making Independence Work
24. Quoted in Coogan, *Ireland Since the Rising,* p. 62.

25. Quoted in Coogan, *Ireland Since the Rising,* p. 65.

26. Quoted in Neville, *A Traveler's History of Ireland,* p. 209.

27. Quoted in Coogan, *Ireland Since the Rising,* p. 65.

28. Quoted in Connery, *The Irish,* p. 145.

29. Quoted in Neville, *A Traveler's History of Ireland,* p. 196.

30. Quoted in Neville, *A Traveler's History of Ireland,* p. 200.

Chapter Five: Renewed Conflict
31. Quoted in Neville, *A Traveler's History of Ireland,* p. 226.

Chapter Six: Ireland at a Crossroad
32. Quoted in Jack Holland, *Hope Against History.* New York: Henry Holt, 1999, p. 175.

33. Quoted in Holland, *Hope Against History,* p. 175.

34. Quoted in Holland, *Hope Against History,* p. 195.

35. Quoted in Thomas J. O'Hanlon, *The Irish.* New York: Harper and Row, 1975, p. 267.

Chronology

B.C.

ca. 6000
Ireland is settled by Mesolithic people.

ca. 3200
Newgrange passage tomb constructed.

ca. 3000
Neolithic culture begins.

ca. 1800
Bronze Age begins in Ireland.

ca. 500
Celts begin to arrive.

A.D.

401
Pope Celestine commissions Palladius to convert Irish to Christianity.

432
St. Patrick begins work in Ireland.

795
Viking invasions begin.

1169
The English land in Ireland.

1366
Statutes of Kilkenny forbid English to marry Irish, speak Gaelic, or wear Irish clothing.

1534–1537
"Silken Thomas" Fitzgerald leads revolt against English.

1607
The Flight of the Earls occurs.

1609
Protestant settlers begin plantation of Ulster.

1641
Irish participate in Ulster revolt that becomes known as the Protestant Massacre.

1649
Oliver Cromwell leads troops through Ireland.

1791
Theobald Wolfe Tone founds United Irishmen.

1793
Catholics regain right to vote and hold office, except in Parliament.

1801
Act of Union makes Ireland part of United Kingdom.

1823
Daniel O'Connell forms Catholic Association.

1828
O'Connell is elected to Parliament despite ban on Catholics holding office.

1829
English Parliament lifts all restrictions on Catholics.

1845–1849
Great Famine kills more than 1 million; another million emigrate.

1848
Young Ireland revolt is crushed by British.

1858
Irish Republican Brotherhood (Fenians) is formed.

1875
Charles Stewart Parnell is elected to Parliament.

1884
Gaelic Athletic Association is founded.

1893
Gaelic League is founded.

1908
Sinn Féin party is founded.

1916
British troops put down Easter Rising; subsequent executions solidify Irish opposition to Britain.

1919
Sinn Féin wins majority of Ireland's seats in Parliament, proclaims Irish republic, and establishes the Dáil Éirann.

1919–1921
Anglo-Irish War.

1920
On November 21, known as Bloody Sunday, a total of 36 people die in raids first by the IRA and then by the Black and Tans.

1921
Anglo-Irish Treaty signed in London.

1922–1923
Irish fight civil war over treaty with Britain.

1937
Irish constitution is approved.

1949
Republic of Ireland proclaims itself free of all connection with Britain.

1968
Protest marchers in Londonderry are attacked by police; incident is beginning of "the Troubles."

1972
British troops in Londonderry kill thirteen protest marchers on "Bloody Sunday"; British impose direct rule of Northern Ireland.

1973
Republic of Ireland joins European Union.

1985
Anglo-Irish agreement calls for cooperation of Britain and the Irish Republic in seeking solution in Northern Ireland.

1994

IRA calls cease-fire; Sinn Féin president Gerry Adams meets with government officials; President Bill Clinton allows Adams to visit United States.

1995

Sinn Féin leader Gerry Adams withdraws from peace talks; IRA ends cease-fire; U.S. president Clinton promises to work for peace in Northern Ireland; George Mitchell is named to chair peace commission.

1997

IRA calls second cease-fire.

1998

(April 10) All parties sign Good Friday agreement; (May 22) voters in north and south overwhelmingly endorse Good Friday agreement; (June 25) first Assembly elected in Northern Ireland.

2001

IRA begins decomissioning its weapons.

For Further Reading

Giovanni Costigan, *A History of Modern Ireland*. New York: Pegasus, 1969. A book about Irish history up to the 1930s, with a heavy emphasis on pre–free state history.

Mike Cronin, *A History of Ireland*. New York: Palgrave, 2001. Another book about Irish history, with an emphasis on early Ireland.

K.S. Daly, *Ireland*. Berkeley, CA: Ten Speed, 1994. A book with many offbeat encyclopedic entries about Ireland and the Irish people.

Alvin Jackson, *Ireland, 1798–1998*. Oxford, England: Blackwell, 1999. A book that traces the history of Ireland from just before Theobald Wolfe Tone's rebellion to modern times.

Micheál MacLiammóir, *Ireland*. New York: Viking, 1966. Another oversized book with plenty of pictures of Ireland and historical text.

Works Consulted

J.C. Beckett, *The Making of Modern Ireland.* New York: Alfred A. Knopf, 1966. A dated but still interesting story of Ireland's history until the mid-1960s.

Donald S. Connery, *The Irish.* New York: Simon and Schuster, 1968. A book about the many oddities of Irish life, dated but still interesting.

Timothy Patrick Coogan, *Ireland Since the Rising.* New York: Frederick A. Praeger, 1966. A history of Ireland since the Easter Rising.

Constantine Fitzgibbon, *The Life and Times of Eamon De Valera.* New York: Macmillan, 1973. A comprehensive biography of Eamon De Valera.

R.F. Foster, ed., *The Oxford Illustrated History of Ireland.* Oxford, England: Oxford University Press, 1989. A very detailed history of Ireland.

Tony Gray, *The Irish Answer.* Boston: Little, Brown, 1966. A book covering Irish history until the mid-1960s.

Jack Holland, *Hope Against History.* New York: Henry Holt, 1999. An examination of the conflict in Northern Ireland, including the Good Friday peace agreement.

Michael L. Landon, *Erin and Britannia.* Chicago: Nelson-Hall, 1981. A book detailing the historical background between Great Britain and Ireland until 1922.

Oliver MacDonagh, *Ireland.* Englewood Cliffs, NJ: Prentice-Hall, 1968. A book detailing Irish history from the union of

Britain and Ireland to the mid-1960s.

Magnus Magnusson, *Landlord or Tenant?* London: Bodley Head, 1978. A look at Irish history up to the country's partition in the 1920s.

Dervla Murphy, *Ireland.* Salem, NH: Salem House, 1985. An oversize book with many pictures of Ireland and text about its history.

Peter Neville, *A Traveler's History of Ireland.* New York: Interlink Books, 1997. A book about the history of Ireland, including its many literary figures.

Thomas J. O'Hanlon, *The Irish.* New York: Harper and Row, 1975. A book about the many facets of Irish life.

Fintan O'Toole, *The Lie of the Land.* New York: Verso, 1997. A book of essays about modern Irish life.

Index

Abbey Theatre, 50
Act of Union, 24
Acts of Uniformity and Su-
    premacy, 21
Adams, Gerry, 91
Ahern, Bertie, 94
American Revolution, 23
Anglicanism, 16, 17
Anglo-Irish Agreement, 85–86
an taoiseach. *See* taoiseach
Arnold, Matthew, 14
Auxiliaries, 47–49

Black and Tans, 47–49
Blair, Tony, 93
Bloody Sunday, 49, 78–79
border, 51
Boundary Commission, 61, 62
British Commonwealth, 52–53
Brooke, Peter, 89
Bruce, Edward, 14
Bruce, Robert, 14
Butt, Isaac, 31

Carson, Edward, 36, 38–39
Casement, Roger, 40, 41, 44
Catholic Association, 26
Catholic Church
    constitution of Republic of Ire-
        land and, 66–67
    importance of, to peasants,
        18–19
    opposition to violence in Ire-
        land and, 37–38
    repression of, by English,
        20–21
    see also Northern Ireland; Re-
        public of Ireland

Catholic Emancipation Act, 27
Catholic rent, 26
Celestine (pope), 11
Celts, 10
Chamberlain, Neville, 68
Chichester-Clark, James Dawson,
    76
Church of England, 15, 16
    see also Anglicanism; Protes-
        tantism
Citizen Army, 37
civil war, 54–58
Clinton, Bill, 91–92, 93
Collins, Michael, 46, 53, 54, 55,
    62, 68
commonwealth. *See* British Com-
    monwealth
Confession (St. Patrick), 12
Connolly, James, 40
Conservative Party, 34–35, 39
constitution, 66–67
Cosgrave, W.T., 57–58, 62
Costello, John Aloysius, 71, 72,
    73
Council of Ireland, 79–80
Craig, James, 59, 70
Cromwell, Oliver, 21–22

Dáil Éirann (lower house of Irish
    Parliament), 45, 46, 53–54
Davitt, Michael, 32
Democratic Unionist Party, 95
depression, 67
De Valera, Eamon
    boycotts and, 58, 61
    Catholic Church and, 64
    importance of, 63, 64
    imprisonment of, 44–45, 46

nationalism of, 44–45
Nazi Germany and, 70
negotiations with England and, 46, 52, 53–54
oath of allegiance and, 63, 65
partition and, 61
peace treaty and, 55–56
trade negotiation and, 68
see also Irish Free State; Republic of Ireland; Sinn Féin
discrimination
religious, and warfare, 21, 27, 57
dominion status, 53, 62–63
draft. *See* military conscription

"Easter 1916" (Yeats), 50
Easter Rising of 1916, 39, 40–42, 43, 64
Edward (king of England), 16–17
Éirann (original inhabitants of Ireland), 10
Éire (Ireland), 10, 65
Elizabeth I (queen of England), 17
England
conquest of Ireland, 13–14
early Irish rebellions against, 14–15
IRA terrorism in, 79
political parties of, 34–35
Erin (Ireland), 10
European Union (EU), 83

famine, 28–31
Faulkner, Brian, 80
Fenians, 20–21
Fianna Fáil (political party), 63, 64, 65, 71
FitzGerald, Garret, 84
Fitzgerald, Gerald, 17
Fitzgerald, Gerald Óg, 14
Flight of the Earls, 17
Four Courts, 54
French Revolution, 23

Gaelic Athletic Association, 34

Gaelic Celts. *See* Celts
Gaelic culture, 15
Gaelic language, 65
Gaelic League, 34
George V (king of England), 51
Gladstone, William, 32–33, 67
Gonne, Maud, 50
Good Friday peace agreement, 93–95
Great Britain. *See* England
Griffith, Arthur, 37, 45, 52, 54, 55

Henry VIII (king of England), 14–16
Home Government Association (HGA), 31
home rule, 31, 33, 37–38
Home Rule League (HRL), 31, 32
House of Commons, 24, 34–35
House of Lords, 35
Hume, John, 95

Incompatibles, The (Arnold), 14
IRA. *See* Irish Republican Army
Ireland
Catholic Church and, 16–17
conversion to Christianity of, 11–13
counties (former kingdoms) of, 10
division into two countries by English Parliament, 49–51
English conquest of, 13–14
land ownership in, 15, 16, 17–18, 22, 31–34
nickname, 13
population changes in, 22–23, 28
pre-Christian history of, 10–11
rebellions against English, 14–15, 17
religious differences in, 18–19
Scotland and, 14
union with Great Britain and, 24–25
Viking invasions of, 13

see also Irish Free State; Republic of Ireland
Irish Free State
  civil war in, 54–58, 59–62
  creation of, 53
  depression and, 67
  dominion status and, 53
  economic problems of, 67–71
  emigration and, 69
  government of, 61
  independence and, 71
  isolationism and, 67
  leadership of, 57–58, 63–65
  manufacturing and, 69
  neutrality of, 70–71
  partition of, 71
  prime minister of, 65
  unemployment and, 67
  United States and, 46
  World War II and, 70–71
  see also Ireland; Republic of Ireland
Irish National Party, 39
Irish Parliament, 31
  see also Irish Free State; Republic of Ireland
Irish Parliamentary Party, 38–39
Irish Question, 43
Irish Renaissance, 50
Irish republic. *See* Republic of Ireland
Irish Republican Army (IRA)
  bombings and, 79
  Catholic Church and, 83–85
  cease-fire and, 89–90
  hunger strikes and, 81
  Irish government and, 73
  organization and early activity of, 46–49
  peace negotiations and, 90–95
  terrorist activities of, 87–88, 93
Irish Republican Brotherhood (IRB), 30–31, 37, 40
Irish Unionist Party, 36
Irish Volunteers, 37

James I (king of England), 17
Johnson, Samuel, 97
Johnston, James, 18

Kennedy, Edward, 91

Land Act of 1831, 32–33
Land League, 31–34
League of Nations, 62
Lemass, Sean, 72, 73
Letter to the Soldiers of Coroticus (St. Patrick), 12
Liberal Party, 34–35, 39, 43–44
Lloyd George, David, 43, 45, 47, 49

Major, John, 89, 93
Mary (queen of England), 15–16
Mayhew, Patrick, 89, 90–91
military conscription, 44
Mitchell, George, 92–94
monasteries, 12–13
Mountbatten, Louis, 81
nationalism, 25, 47
  see also Irish Republican Army; Orangemen; Sinn Féin; Unionist Party
naval bases, 53
Northern Ireland
  Anglo-Irish Agreement and, 86
  Bloody Sunday and, 78–79
  border of, after partition, 51, 60–62
  British military in, 77, 78–79
  Catholics in, 59, 60–61, 70, 78–79
  cease-fire and, 89
  civil liberties and, 94
  civil war in, 54–58
  counties of, 35, 50
  economic growth in, 73
  education in, 73
  factories in, 68
  government agencies of, 86
  hunger strikes and, 81
  industries in, 71
  IRA activity in, 59, 60, 73,

81–82
land ownership in, 17–18
majority rule and, 95
militias in, 75
peace negotiations and, 90–95
political parties of, 36, 95
poverty in, 70
Protestant settlement of, 17–18
Protestants in, 59, 60, 66–67
religious discrimination in, 70, 75–76, 77–78
separation from Republic of Ireland, 49–51
social welfare in, 73
strikes in, 80
violence in, 77–79
Northern Ireland Parliament, 51, 58
North-South Council, 94

oath of allegiance, 53
O'Brien, Father John A., 30
O'Connell, Daniel, 25–26, 27
O'Higgins, Kevin, 57–58, 68
Oireachtas (Irish Parliament), 65
O'Neill, Hugh, 17
O'Neill, Shane, 17
O'Neill, Terence, 73, 75–76
Orangemen, 36
O'Shea, Henry, 33
O'Shea, Kitty, 33

Paisley, Ian, 73, 76, 95
Pale, the (English-controlled part of Ireland), 17
Palladius, 11–12
Parliament (English), 24, 27, 31, 34–35, 44, 47, 56
Parliament (Irish), 31
see also Dáil Éirann; Seanad Éireann
Parliament (Northern Ireland). See Northern Ireland Parliament
Parnell, Charles Stewart, 31–34, 39
partition, 49–51

see also Northern Ireland; Republic of Ireland
peace agreement, 93–95
peace conference, 52
peace negotiations, 79–80, 90–95
Pearse, Patrick, 40–42
peasants, 18, 19, 23
Penal Laws, 21
Pitt, William, 24, 25
Plunket, Oliver, 19
political parties. See Orangemen; Sinn Féin; Unionist Party; other individual party names
Potato Famine, 28–31
Protestant Church, 24
Protestantism, 21–22
see also Anglicanism
Protestant Massacre, 21
Protestants, 17, 35–36
see also Church of England
Protestant Unionist Party. See Unionist Party
Provos (Provisional IRA), 77–78, 79, 87–88
see also Irish Republican Army; nationalism

Redmond, John, 38–39
religion. See Anglicanism; Catholic Church; Protestants
religious differences, 18–19
religious discrimination and warfare. See discrimination.
Repeal Association, 27
Republic of Ireland
agriculture in, 68–69
border with Northern Ireland, 51
Catholic Church and, 83–86, 96
censorship in, 84
diversification and, 96–97
divorce in, 84, 96
economic progress and, 96–97
future of, 97
government relationship with

IRA and, 82–83
independence and, 71
modernization and, 83, 96–97
partition and, 71
peace negotiations and, 95
poverty in, 72
religion in, 74
secularization of, 84–85, 96
see also Ireland; Irish Free
State
Royal Irish Constabulary (RIC), 46
Royal Ulster Constabulary
(RUC), 59–60

Scotland, 14, 17
Seanad Éireann, 65
Shaw, George Bernard, 42
"Silken Thomas," 14
Sinn Féin (We Ourselves)
effect of Easter Rising on, 42,
43
goal of, 34
growth of, 44–47
Home Rule Bill of 1912 and,
37
Irish Free State and, 57–58
opposition of, to British con-
trol, 37
U.S. recognition of, 91–92
Smith, Jean Kennedy, 91
Social Democratic and Labour
Party, 95
Society of United Irishmen,
23–24
Spain, 20–21
Spenser, Edmund, 19

Statute of Westminster, 63
Statutes of Kilkenny, 13, 15
St. Patrick (patron saint of Ire-
land), 12
Sunningdale agreement, 79–80

taoiseach (prime minister of Ireland), 65, 71, 72, 73
terrorism, 48–49, 54–57
Thatcher, Margaret, 81, 85
Tone, Theobald Wolfe, 23–24
trade war, 67–71
treaty of 1921, 53–54
Trimble, David, 94, 95
"troubles, the," 47–58
tuath (ancient Irish kingdom), 10

Ulster. *See* Northern Ireland
Ulster Defense Association, 88
Ulster Plantation, 17
Ulster Volunteer Force, 36, 37
Ulster Worker's Council, 80
unemployment, 67
Unionist Party, 50, 56, 75, 87–88,
89, 95
United States, 46, 91–93

Vikings, 13
violence, 48–49, 54–55, 56–57

Whitaker, Kenneth, 72
Wilson, Henry, 54
World War I, 38–39
World War II, 70–71

Yeats, William Butler, 50

Picture Credits

About the Author

Russell Roberts graduated from Rider University in Lawrenceville, New Jersey. A full-time freelance writer, he has published over two hundred articles and short stories and over a dozen books. He currently resides in Bordentown, New Jersey, with his family and a conniving cat named Rusti.